MAX STEINER'S *NOW, VOYAGER*

Max Steiner at the piano, 1947. Courtesy of Photographic Archives, Harold B. Lee Library, Brigham Young University, Provo, Utah.

MAX STEINER'S *NOW, VOYAGER*
A Film Score Guide

KATE DAUBNEY

Film Score Guides, Number 1

Greenwood Press
Westport, Connecticut • London

Library of Congress Cataloging-in-Publication Data

Daubney, Kate, 1969–
    Max Steiner's Now, voyager : a film score guide, / Kate Daubney.
      p. cm.—(Film score guides, ISSN 1527-7291 ; no. 1)
    Includes bibliographical references and index.
    ISBN 0–313–31253–2 (alk. paper)
    1. Steiner, Max, 1888–1971. Now, voyager. I. Title: Now, voyager. II. Title.
    III. Series.
  ML410.S8163 D38   2000
  781.5′42—dc21   99–088601

British Library Cataloguing in Publication Data is available.

Library of Congress Catalog Card Number: 99–088601
ISBN: 0–313–31253–2
ISSN: 1527–7291

First published in 2000

Greenwood Press, 88 Post Road West, Westport, CT 06881
An imprint of Greenwood Publishing Group, Inc.
www.greenwood.com

Printed in the United States of America

Copyright Acknowledgment

The author and publisher gratefully acknowledge permission for use of the following material:

Max Steiner, *Notes to You*. Unpublished Autobiography, held as part of the Max Steiner Collection,
Arts and Communications Archive, Harold B. Lee Library, Brigham Young University, 1963–65.

To B. and family

CONTENTS

FIGURES

PREFACE

Between 1988, when I began my first tentative explorations into the music of Max Steiner as an undergraduate, and now, the publication of my first book on the subject, the study of film music has taken a massive stride forward. At the end of the 1980s, Claudia Gorbman's *Unheard Melodies* had just been published, the first thorough theorisation of an approach to understanding the way music operates in film. It took its place beside a small selection of historical and biographical chronicles: Roy Prendergast's *Film Music: A Neglected Art*, Tony Thomas's *Film Score* and *Music for the Movies*, Christopher Palmer's *The Composer in Hollywood*. During the early 1990s, while I was researching my doctoral thesis on Steiner's scores composed between 1939 and 1945, Kathryn Kalinak picked up Gorbman's narrative train of thought and applied it to a more focused area, the 'classical' Hollywood score. Royal S. Brown brought his detailed perspective on Bernard Herrmann to bear on the reading of all film scores as part of a multiplicity of musical canons in *Overtones and Undertones*, while William Darby and Jack Du Bois in *American Film Music* gave a thorough guided tour to the chief scores and composers from 1915 to 1990. Most recently Russell Lack has unearthed the buried history of film music in *24 Frames Under* (1997).

The variety of these and other texts, and the role they played in developing film musicology as an academic discipline, with connections and references to its related studies and '-ologies,' show how diverse the investigation can be and how much has to be taken into account in an ever-increasing body of scholarship. Yet, in defining the discipline, attention has been given to marking out the boundaries and dealing separately with historical, theoretical and biographical practices. The Greenwood Series of Film Score Guides begins the process of looking within, drawing the different practices together in order to look in full at one score from every angle, instead of all scores from one angle: it also enables scholars to manage the technical, idiomatic and historical changes in scoring practice without resorting to the reconstruction of the theories and applications.

Furthermore, the need to justify the scholarship has evolved into a question of what should be done with it now that it exists: there is no better use than to pinpoint individual scores that have played a significant role in how composers write film music, in the way audiences hear it, in directorial perceptions of it, and in how scholars have theorised about it. The Series is, similarly, intended to reflect the variety of people who enjoy, experience and understand film music, drawing together contextual and experiential ideas with academic concepts of film studies and critical and analytical musicology. The Series Guides can be used in an academic context to support courses on film music, but they can also be enjoyed for their insight into the individual scores which have formed the love of film music experienced by many.

Acknowledgements

I am indebted to many people who have supported me in the writing of this book, and my brief thanks here will, I hope, go a little way toward compensating them for their greatly appreciated tolerance and understanding.

My principal thanks go to Dr. James V. D'Arc, curator of the Film Music Archives in the Harold B. Lee Library at Brigham Young University, Utah, in which the Max Steiner Collection is held. He has been consistently supportive since I first approached him for archival assistance in 1990, and he has made the resources of the Collection and its parent archive available to me most generously. His enthusiasm for the music of Steiner is clearly manifested in the excellent presentation of the Collection and of the recent Collection Catalogue, and I am extremely grateful for all the extra information he has imparted to me in the course of more than eight years of letters and conversation. In the same vein, Edward Leaney, an enthusiast and dedicated scholar of Steiner, has been generous to a fault in providing me with material about Steiner's pre-Hollywood career from his own painstaking research. Louise Klos Steiner Elian, Max Steiner's third wife, was kind enough to consent to be interviewed, and I am grateful for her honesty and her attention to detail.

I would like to thank Thomas Wells, photoarchivist at the Harold B. Lee Library, Brigham Young University, who made the photographic transparencies of the scores which I have used for much of my research of Steiner's work. I am also grateful to Susan Corrigan and the staff of the Imaging Technology Centre at Brigham Young University for the high quality reproduction of the score page from *Now, Voyager* used in Chapter 2. Leon Skelton at IMP Ltd. was extremely helpful in organising the necessary copyright permission for reproduction of Steiner's scores in this book.

I am grateful for the support of my colleagues in the Department of Music at the University of Leeds, particularly David Cooper whose perspective has been invaluable. Pamela St. Clair and Lisa Webber, my editors at Greenwood Press, have been very supportive, and I would be adrift without the practical and intellectual inputs of Lesley Jones and Liz Kane.

Many of the ideas I have brought to this book arose from ways in which I have sought to teach and explain Max Steiner's approach to film scoring on a variety of undergraduate film music courses. This book, and the Series to which it belongs, evolved because of those courses, and with feedback from all the students I have taught on them: I owe them thanks for sharing in my zeal.

INTRODUCTION

Now, Voyager (1942) is a film of striking significance: the escapism of early 1940s' cinema finds a feminist agenda, brought to the forefront of public awareness by one of Hollywood's biggest stars, against a wash of gloriously rich and expressive music. Max Steiner won an Academy Award for his score for the film; yet, unlike the films for which he received his other two Awards—*The Informer* (1935) and *Since You Went Away* (1944)—*Now, Voyager* had not been heavily commended in other categories in the selection process. Steiner's was one of only three nominations for the film, the other two going to Bette Davis for Best Actress, and Gladys Cooper for Best Supporting Actress, neither of whom won their category, despite giving among the most distinctive performances of their careers and the era. The score is, however, one of Steiner's greatest, and it stands out in a career spanning over thirty years and over three hundred films: it combines his understanding of drama with a fluency of melodic statement and development, drawing the whole score together in a way which he would never surpass.

Steiner's approach, in the majority of scores, was to capture the elements of the film's story in a number of musical themes, with a broad vocabulary of melody and instrumentation which matched the range of story genres for which he composed. Most often, he used themes to delineate the characters in a story, but above all he designed and conceived his music as adding something to the film, not just underscoring it or merging into the background. This might appear to be at odds with his frequently stated contention that a score should never be disruptive to the audience's concentration, yet he viewed the very existence of music in a film as an opportunity for it to be as influential as the other narrative components. The origins of this ideology of film composition have been chronicled as much for their part in the formative years of sound film scoring techniques as for their place in the development of Steiner's own idiom. The former, however, often takes precedence over the latter, with Steiner's early scores being seen as more influential over the stylistic developments of his contemporaries in Hollywood, than on his own evolution. As early as 1933, with the enormously successful score for *King Kong*, he had a good sense of which elements in a film would benefit from musical accompaniment, but there is surprising evidence of the features of his mature film scoring style in the musical forms of his pre-Hollywood career. Chapter 1 explores the context and experiences from which Steiner's approach emerged, and Chapter 2 considers the distinctive features of this style, particularly as they appear in his score for *Now, Voyager*.

While the score may influence readings of the film, it is also interesting to consider how readings of the film might have influenced the composition of the score, and the analysis of Steiner's music can take place in a range of critical and historical contexts. *Now, Voyager* is a fascinating document of both Hollywood and American preoccupations with women's lives and the issues which were perceived to be important to them: love, family, work, social purpose. The film invites complex, sometimes conflicting readings of the central character as a vamp-ish adultress and displaced mother, and the narrative is dominated by strongly drawn female characters. Chapter 3 considers the context in which the film was created, the range of influences over its production, and how these elements are manifested in readings and interpretations. Chapter 4 considers an experiential view of the film's music and similarities with the sound of other contemporary Steiner scores. The critical reception of the music is also explored alongside the influence of this score on more recent canons of film musicology.

This range of critical, historical and interpretative readings and perspectives creates a rich context in which to analyse the score. The juxtaposition of musical analysis with narrative schemes exposes Steiner's dual intention: his thematic design for the score seems superficially to emphasise the dominance of characterisation, while concealing a far deeper scheme of thematic coherence, created by motif, tonality and orchestration. The analysis, Chapter 5, adopts what is likely to have been Steiner's own approach to composition and considers exactly how his understanding of music's dramatic function is manifested in this score. Valuable evidence for analysis is found in Steiner's short score for this film, both in the musical notation and the margin notes and annotations; the examples given are all taken from the original manuscript. The scores for his other films composed in this period give further evidence of Steiner's scoring practice, and his letters and scrapbooks and the unpublished autobiography, *Notes to You*, all contribute the composer's own perspective to a broader debate about how scores are interpreted. All of the primary resource material is from the Max Steiner Collection in the Arts and Communications Archive at Brigham Young University.

— Chapter 1 —

MAX STEINER'S
MUSICAL BACKGROUND

Film music composition could be seen as Max Steiner's second career. He was 41 when he went to Hollywood in 1929, called to the burgeoning world of cinema from a successful career as a musical director and arranger on Broadway. Unlike his contemporaries, particularly Erich Korngold, Steiner's background was not in the 'high art' of fin-de-siècle Viennese music, but in the harsher economic practicalities of entertainment theatre: twenty-five years of such experience would turn out to be an invaluable preparation for the constraints of Hollywood music-making. The extent of his involvement in the evolution of film scoring practice and the adoption of his techniques by other composers suggest that Steiner came to cinema scoring with a master plan for how the newest art form might benefit from one of the oldest. It was, however, as much circumstance as design which fostered the connection between Steiner's musical theatre and cinematic careers and led to the achievements of one of Hollywood's most prolific composers. Steiner's facility for melodic writing and instrumentation, the technique which characterises the score for *Now, Voyager*, has been widely admired and copied, yet it can be traced from his pre-Hollywood experiences and the idioms of his musical background.

A VIENNESE CHILDHOOD

Musical theatre was a form of apprenticeship in the Steiner family, and it is no surprise that Max's career began in this field. The family were central to Viennese culture in the late nineteenth century: in his unpublished autobiography *Notes to You*, Steiner remarks that "[t]he world of the theater that was opened up to me at an early age was the real thrill of my life, and the source of my inspiration."[1] His paternal grandfather, also called Maximilian, had been a director of the Theater an der Wien in the 1870s, one of the most important theatres in Vienna, having provided a venue for the premiere of the first version of Beethoven's *Fidelio* in 1805. In the 1850s, imminent bankruptcy was averted by a change in emphasis from concert hall music to the melodious Parisian operetta of Offenbach and later to the Viennese operetta of Johann Strauss II and Franz Lehár.[2] It has been suggested that Maximilian Steiner was directly responsible for encouraging Strauss to compose operetta, after Strauss's first wife, Jetty Treffz, brought to him music by her husband, which the director matched with lyrics.[3] Steiner was not able to stage Strauss's *Die lustigen Weiber von Wien*, which was completed in 1869, but he continued his involvement with Strauss, to the extent that he was credited with the "arrangement" of the libretto for *Indigo und die vierzig Räuber* (1871).[4]

The Hollywood Steiner, christened Maximilian Raoul Walter, was born in May 1888. His father, Gabor, was a theatre manager and was responsible for building the Riesenrad Ferris Wheel in the theme park "Venice in Vienna." Max's mother, Maria, was a chorus girl at the Theater an der Wien when she met Gabor. There were many opportunities for Max Steiner to compose during his childhood in theatrical Vienna, and works from this period include marches for regimental bands and some hit songs for a show staged by his father. Gabor Steiner was a great motivation for his son, providing a context for performance as well as encouragement.[5] Max describes his first piano lessons:

When I was six years old I took three or four piano lessons a week. I hated it. Bach, Beethoven, Czerney [sic] and five-fingered exercises bored me. I rebelled and my father had to give me a Kronen for every lesson I took. . . . To escape from the boredom of my lessons with my first teacher I often improvised at the piano with more modern music of my own. Papa would always encourage me by saying "Write it down. Write it down!"[6]

Steiner goes on to suggest that his experience of improvisation may have prepared his musical tastes: "[p]erhaps this is why some years later in my early teens I was able to understand and appreciate the music of Debussy which was Avant Garde [sic] for those days."[7]

Steiner's musical training was both academic and circumstantial: on a formal level he was admitted to the Vienna Imperial Academy of Music[8] at the age of 15, "where by the Grace of God and excellent instruction I completed the required four years in one and was accorded the honor of being the best student in the academy."[9] He lists his teachers as: Herman Graedner, harmony and orchestration; Robert Fuchs, counterpoint; Felix Weingartner, composition; Professor Josef Brenner, organ; Professor Wottawa, brass; Edmund Eysler, piano.[10] Steiner notes that his instrumental strength was the piano, although there is a sense of the broader advantage of other instrumental lessons: "it was enough for me to know what the instrument could do."[11] An early influence over Steiner's melodic style could be found in the music of Eysler, whose first operetta, *Bruder Straubinger*, was produced at the Theater an der Wien in 1903, the same year Steiner began at the Imperial Academy. Traubner describes Eysler's operettas as often having poor libretti, in a simple style, with songs often drawing on another popular Viennese form, the waltz.[12] In his later attempts at writing works for musical theatre, Steiner was keen to try his hand at libretto writing, often with minimal success; more significantly the waltz is a recurrent melodic form in the themes of his film scores—for example *Dark Victory* (1939), *In This Our Life* (1941) and *Now, Voyager* (1942).

Steiner may also have been influenced by Weingartner, who conducted and directed the Vienna Opera from 1908 to 1911. Although he studied composition with Weingartner, Steiner also notes, "I never thought of myself as a composer, but dreamed only of becoming a great conductor."[13] He began early, in 1900 at the age of 12, when he was allowed to conduct the Viennese premiere of Gustave Kerker's operetta *Die Schöne von New York* (*The Belle of New York*) at his father's theatre.[14] It might seem that Steiner's 'theatrical inspiration' would be restricted to composition, but the conducting reflects his interest in the broader view of what music can do in a theatrical context. Steiner notes that much of his conducting knowledge came from watching the rehearsals for shows and that the practical experience gained from his family and social circumstances consolidated his academic education:

I became familiar with the sounds of an orchestra and what could be done with it. This was the training which many years later was to lead me to Hollywood. I was credited at the time with originating some effects in the orchestra which are now routine, such as muted brass with the strings underneath; woodwinds below the brass and other musical effects which were innovations at that time.[15]

In *Notes to You*, Steiner goes into detail about the types of orchestra to be heard in late nineteenth century Vienna, an attention and precision to the combination of instruments which was typical of his approach to scoring. In particular, he describes the line-ups of the Austrian Army regimental bands which his father hired to play in his theme park, the operetta orchestras used in the open-air summer theatre, and the predominantly string based "Salon orchestra [which] was especially suited to the Viennese waltzes and polkas."[16] The descriptions show not only an interest in the combination of instruments used to create a particular style, but also the numbers of personnel in each part. For example, for the summer operetta orchestras, "a little heavier sound was required. . . 12 first violins; 6 second violins; four violas; 3 celli and 3 basses; two oboe[s] and four horns."[17]   Throughout his professional life as both musical director and composer, Steiner maintained this strong sense of exactly how many individual instruments would be needed to create the sound he sought, for both standard orchestrations and more unusual ensembles.[18]

Aside from his early engagement with Kerker's *Die Schöne von New York*, Steiner's other main contact with the world of operetta was through Franz Lehár, who Steiner recalls as working for a time as a military bandmaster for Steiner's father, Gabor.[19]   Certainly, Lehár conducted his own works *Wiener Frauen* (*Viennese Women*) and *Der Rastelbinder* (*The Tinker*) at the Theater an der Wien and at the Carltheater in 1902, following his military band career. *Die lustige Witwe* (*The Merry Widow*) was to be his most successful work: its fluent melodies characterised the romantic plot, and the love duets in waltz idioms surfaced again in Lehár's other works as well as in the operettas of many of his Viennese contemporaries, such as Emmerich Kálmán, Oscar Straus and Leo Fall.[20]   Steiner paid his own tribute to Lehár through a pastiche which he composed entitled *Der lustige Witwer* (*The Merry Widower*), which was staged in 1907 at Danzers Orpheum in Vienna; in the same year Steiner's short operetta *Die schöne Griechin* (*The Beautiful Greek Girl*), with libretto by Julius Wilhelm, was also staged.[21]

MUSICAL THEATRE: EUROPE AND BROADWAY

Between 1907 and 1914, Steiner travelled frequently between Britain and Europe to work on different theatrical productions, although precise dates are difficult to find because of the vagueness of the autobiography and the lack of adequate corroborative evidence.[22] His father's considerable financial problems forced Max to leave Vienna, although he returned in 1911 to try to appease the creditors.[23] Between 1907 and 1911, he worked in British musical theatre: his first job was on *The Girls of Gottenburg*, composed by Ivan Caryll and Lionel Monckton, and he so impressed theatrical promoter George Dance at the dress rehearsal that the impresario put him onto the London production of *Véronique*, which Steiner describes as Dance's biggest show. After a period of working as musical director for shows at a number of London theatres, including the London Palladium, the Tivoli, the Adelphi, the Empire and the Hippodrome, he joined John Tiller, who was manager of the Tiller Girls. Steiner composed a ballet for the troupe, *Amsterdam*, which was performed in Paris, Ireland and all over England, and another "Irish Ballet" entitled *Killarney*, again produced by Tiller.[24] He also describes writing and arranging songs for some of the vaudeville and comedy stars of the day, including Alice Lloyd, Eugene Stratton, Fred Emney and George Robey.[25] The most substantial project he undertook was a show entitled *Topsy Turvy*, which was set on a forgotten Pacific island where male and female roles were reversed. Steiner composed the music for this show, and the libretto was written by a friend, Raoul Lurion: he notes, "Needless to say, the show was not a big success. In fact, it was very mediocre and ran only four weeks in London. Lurion's father who had financed it, lost so much money that he closed the show."[26]

During this period in Britain, Steiner returned periodically to Vienna, taking a variety of performing acts back to help out with the financial situation brought on by the collapse of his father's business. He recalls producing his own opera, *Der Kristalpokall (The Crystal Cup)*, which had a cast of two, to minimal acclaim, but he notes that Julius Korngold, father of Erich Wolfgang Korngold, wrote a critical review of the work: "He called me a genius, said the orchestrations were great, the composition wonderful, but the book was lousy. (I wrote it myself)."[27] In the spring of 1912, Steiner returned to London as musical director of an American revue entitled *Come Over Here*, which starred Fanny Brice and the Tiller Girls and which ran for over a year into 1914. It was followed by a period with a staged circus and then with another American show called *Tillie's Nightmare*, produced by Ned Wayburn. The range of idioms, forms and contexts in which Steiner was composing and arranging is typical of the diversity of early twentieth-century European theatrical entertainment, and it gives an indication of how adaptable he needed to be, a versatility he would rely on in judging the different needs for music in the wide range of film genres which he later scored: musicals, melodramas, historical epics, biographies, westerns, crime dramas.

In this period before the outbreak of World War I, Steiner describes the difficulty of being Austrian or German in Great Britain, which he calls the "tight little isle": in December 1914, finding himself increasingly unwelcome, he left Britain for New York and began his American career.[28] Employment was not easy to come by, however, despite his considerable experience, and this is shown in his autobiography, where Steiner divides the New York years into pre-Broadway and Broadway.[29] The first period covers at least twelve months from the end of 1914 to some time in 1916 when Steiner became involved in his first Broadway musical. During this time he could not get membership of the musicians' union, so he was forced to work at a series of odd jobs loosely related to music entertainment: he began as a copyist for Harms Music Publishing, whose subsidiaries were Boosey and Chappell, and for Waterson, Berlin and Snyder, of whom Irving Berlin was a partner. It appears from the autobiography that Steiner gathered both work and a reputation through a few well chosen acquaintances and through perseverance in various performance environments. In particular, he notes how he loitered at a rehearsal hall on 6th Avenue, helping out as an accompanist, eventually meeting a famous dancing partnership called Adelaide and Hughes. He could not conduct for a show they were doing because he was not eligible to join the union without United States citizenship, but he recalls how eventually he got a non-union job playing with a restaurant orchestra in Coney Island. It was during these early days that Steiner made his first connection with cinema, through a meeting with Samuel L. Rothafel, owner of the Roxy chain of cinemas. He was invited to join the "40-piece non-union orchestra on the stage" of the theatre and describes the work in *Notes to You*:

First, we played the overture. Then we had a scenic short showing beautiful scenery around the world; then there was an act; then the news; another ten minutes and another act; and finally, the feature. The feature picture was partly played by the orchestra, then the organ took over for fifteen minutes. After the feature we had another act and then the comedy which we all played. The program was changed Monday and Thursday. On those two days, on top of everything else, we had a 9 o'clock rehearsal. If this wasn't enough—I had to lay out the music because in those silent days we played printed music and merely made an attempt to fit it to the action as best we could. Of course, it was impossible to catch cues exactly. It wasn't too bad.[30]

Success led to a job as music director for all the theatres on the Fox circuit, and this gained him membership of the musicians' union, although he then returned to musical theatre. He rapidly became involved in a range of Broadway shows, to the extent that he turned down an opportunity to go to Hollywood with Louis Silvers, musical director for Al Jolson, in the early 1920s.

Louis said to me: "Max, with your technique and your knowledge and your spotting of pictures when you were with William Fox, why don't we form a small corporation, go to Hollywood and offer our services to score pictures for any and all. . . . " Lou wanted to write the music where necessary, select and orchestrate it and copy it. He would hire a music editor to cut tracks, hire the orchestra and conduct. In other words, we would offer a package deal to the various studios to score a picture in its entirety. In 1923, the first sound-on-film picture, vaudeville shorts, had been demonstrated by Lee de Forest in the Rivoli Theater in New York. Not until 1927 did Warner Bros. present their part-talking picture, THE JAZZ SINGER with Al Jolson. So you can see how far ahead of its time Lou's idea was. But I was not so far-sighted as he. I was unable to go along with the idea. I didn't think there was any future in it. I think now if we had ever put this plan into operation we might have tied up the whole music business in Hollywood. We might also have taken a lot of headaches off the different studios as well as saved them a lot of money.[31]

Musical comedy in America at this time was partly influenced by the European operetta style of Lehár, which can be seen in the works of Victor Herbert, Rudolf Friml and Sigmund Romberg. Richard Traubner suggests that "[p]erhaps influenced by the close-up intimacy and spectacular passion of the hugely popular silent screen, operettas were forced to be increasingly romantic and full-blooded, rather than satiric or comic."[32]   A strong home-grown American idiom was also developing, through the jazz style shows of Youmans, Kern and Gershwin. Steiner's experience in the European idiom gave him an obvious advantage, but his ear for popular taste was developing quickly through his work in vaudeville and revue. Projects such as *George White's Scandals of 1922* and *Ed Wynn's Grab Bag* (1924) required musical directors, such as Steiner, to draw on and be familiar with the most popular instrumental and song styles of the day, in order to keep the revues musically accessible and commercial. The range of forms and idioms of musical theatre with which Steiner was involved suggests that he had gained a reputation for versatility, although the full extent of the projects he was involved in is not clearly known. In *Notes to You* he describes the 'Broadway' years not through the work he did, but through a series of anecdotes about musicians he knew through touring productions he worked on, and there is only the sketchiest detail about dates and places. He places his direct involvement in conducting or musical direction as being the period from 1916 to 1929, recalling that the first musical comedy he conducted on Broadway was *The Masked Model*, which then toured to San Francisco.[33]   On average he seems to have been involved in two or three different productions every year on Broadway, although there may have been travelling productions with which he had temporary engagements also.[34]

Steiner would have found considerable continuity among the styles he was working in, despite their differences, because of his dominant sense of melody. The characteristic waltz styles of operetta numbers were overtaken by syncopated, jazz-style melodies in the witty, lyric-driven songs of Gershwin and Kern; yet a catchy tune was still the definitive feature, and capturing the mood of the theatrical moment was a vital feature of the shows. He was also strongly influenced by the orchestrators whom he knew or worked with, although typically Steiner flavours his opinions with humorous anecdotes rather than analytical comment. His association with Victor Herbert was clearly important to him:

Herbert had been first cellist at the Theater on the Wien under my grandfather and my father. And what a wonderful gentleman and musician he was. I conducted one of his smaller operettas for him which did not do very well.[35] But the interesting thing about the experience for me was to be able to observe what a master of orchestration Victor Herbert was. . . . For example, the maestro taught me that to imitate an oboe, you put the flute and the viola together and let them play in unison. . . . He had a very individual style of orchestrating, with high cellos against the strings. He taught me a little trick—devisi [sic] violins. He used this because of the limited strings we had in those days in a theater orchestra. Herbert put the strings divisi, that is in three parts or four parts as the case might be, on top, and if this didn't have enough, he wrote the strings in two parts, then put the flutes underneath the two parts and the ear could not detect whether the strings were in two parts or four parts.[36]

Stanley Green's assessment of Herbert's work might equally be applied to Steiner's film scoring:

[Herbert] stood alone in raising the standards of theatre music and orchestrations. No matter how pressed he was, [he] always turned out work that revealed great care in both composition and in the way in which the theatre orchestra might best enhance the effectiveness of a score.[37]

The skill of adapting an orchestration to suit the personnel or economic demands of the production was vital to Steiner in his musical theatre career and later became a hallmark of his film scoring technique. In *Notes to You* he recalls the influence of Frank Saddler, an orchestrator whom he knew on Broadway but probably did not often work with, attributing to him the invention of the orchestral design used on Broadway since the 1920s:

He used no horns at all; 8 violins; 4 violas; no second violins. This was, of course, an economy measure by which we saved two men. Otherwise we would have had to have 4 second violins and 2 violas. But Saddler figured that 4 violas would do the same job and they sure did! Then he had two basses and 2 flutes, one oboe, 2 clarinets; 2 bassoons and whatever brass was necessary; a drum and usually, a harp. This arrangement we use even today even in the big orchestras we follow the same combination although we may have 16 violins and 6 violas; 6 cellos, and sometimes no horns at all.[38]

He may also have learnt more than the use of instrumentation from Saddler, for his description of Saddler's workaholism mirrors the lifestyle Steiner would later find himself adopting in Hollywood:

He worked at a bookeeper's [sic] desk, standing up, sometimes all night. He would work for a couple of hours, then sit down, read the newspaper, have a cup of coffee, which he always kept brewing, and then go back to work. He often worked until nine or ten in the morning without going to bed and then went straight to orchestra rehearsal. I learned modern American orchestration from him.[39]

By the end of the 1920s Steiner had built a solid career in musical theatre, conducting and arranging the works of many of the most renowned composers of the period, although he did little original composition, apart from the music for an unsuccessful musical comedy entitled *Peaches*, which was commissioned by George Lederer.[40]   The nature of Steiner's musical background in Vienna, however, had prepared him as much for musical direction as for creativity, and the versatility he learnt in Europe prepared him for Broadway, as well as for his early Hollywood career. As he came from a family which was heavily involved in musical entertainment and grew up in an environment dominated by the melodies of Viennese operetta, Steiner's background was an investment in popular entertainment. Without substantial compositions of his own to assess from this period, some critics have found it difficult to be certain of the origin of the idiom he took to Hollywood: his use of a wide range of conventional orchestral instruments does equate him with the symphonic composers of his generation, but his ability to create that sound using a band of between sixteen and thirty-five players, honed in the theatre pits of Broadway, reveals why he was so useful to Hollywood and why its demands suited him. Clearly, however, the qualities of his film music are rooted in those factors which characterised the music of Viennese and American musical theatre: melody, dramatic effect and instrumental colour. The waltzes and marches which dominated the songs of early twentieth century Viennese operetta, while capturing the meaning of the lyrics and libretto, became songs-without-words in his Hollywood melodies, expressing the dialogue and carrying the narrative.

HOLLYWOOD

Once again my arrival in [a] strange country occurred at Christmastime. It was 1929, the year of the stockmarket crash of all time. . . . The next few years were to be depression years, not only for show biz, but all businesses. 1930, my first year in Hollywood saw the bankruptcy of the Shuberts in New York. Our beloved Palace [Theatre] also gave up the ghost and was wired for sound. Vaudeville was disappearing altogether and by 1931, 45% of the Broadway theaters were dark. This was the unpromising era in which I started my Hollywood career in high spirits.[41]

Steiner went to Hollywood having been the musical director and conductor for the stage production of the operetta *Rio Rita*, which had just been made into one of the early talking pictures. He was invited by Harry Tierney, a composer on the music staff at RKO Studios with whom he had worked on the original Broadway production in 1927, to join the teams who were rearranging the stage musicals for film.[42] Steiner recalls that his first orchestration job was *Dixiana*, and that although there was minimal music in other RKO pictures, he worked with composer and orchestrator Roy Webb on music for three other cheaply made films.

They would give us only a 10-man orchestra for them and sometimes we used printed music and wrote only the few cues that we needed. We were allowed only three hours to record in. We didn't even have time to write the music in score, but were forced to immediately write in the orchestra parts.[43]

The studios were investing heavily in the technology that made talking pictures possible: the inclusion of music in the budget for production was a relatively recent addition, and so value-for-money in this area was essential, particularly as the mechanics of creating a musical sound track were complex and awkward. Steiner's orchestration techniques, developed to make the most of minimal resources in large theatrical arenas, were immediately in demand, as was his experience of collaboration. Steiner saw out his first year at RKO as part of a team of arrangers and orchestrators adapting musicals for film production, but in 1930 this area of production began to decline as studios looked for new types of film to make. Ironically, music had to defend its role in film after a period during which it had been integral.

　　RKO cut back its music department, but Steiner and Roy Webb stayed on a month-to-month basis, without contracts. Steiner describes the fragility of his situation:

RKO decided they didn't want any music in their dramatic pictures. This was motivated not only by the economic factor, but because they had decided you could not have background music unless you showed the source. . . . They felt, therefore, that they had no use for a full music department.[44]

He stayed on at the behest of William Le Baron, who indicated that there might be more musicals coming, although his first full composition job was for the western *Cimarron* in 1930: Steiner was chosen because others were not available and he was not noted in the film credits. Apart from music for the long title sequence, there is only one other substantial cue, but the music is united by a theme whose triadic feel foreshadows the music for later Westerns, such as *The Oklahoma Kid* (1939).[45] The music for the title sequence sounds like a crude advertisement for Steiner's skills, being built from three distinct melodies sequenced together, showing versatility and a range of moods, but its grandeur suits the rather elaborate staging of the credits.

During the early 1930s, Steiner's involvement in other small scoring projects increased steadily, although many were uncredited, but in 1933 he found his first opportunity to compose a substantial dramatic score, when he was brought in to rescue RKO's big budget *King Kong*. The making of the film had virtually bankrupted the studio, yet executives were anxious about how the audience would experience the giant animated ape and gambled on the considerable expense of a full score to aid the fantasy. Retrospectively, Steiner had no doubts: "[i]t was made for music. It was the kind of film that allowed you to do anything and everything, from weird chords and dissonances to pretty melodies."[46] He used a large orchestra, reputedly of 80 musicians costing tens of thousands of dollars, and wrote a lushly orchestrated score dominated by Kong's striking chromatic motif. The film was a huge success, turning fortunes around at RKO and establishing Steiner's credentials. His 1935 score for *The Informer*, for which he won his first Academy Award, expands and develops the techniques he had established for *King Kong*, blending extensive thematic characterisation, mickey-mousing, and references to the cultural setting of the film. He was finding his compositional voice and, after his move to Warner Brothers in 1936, he began to take more responsibility for the principal scoring of films and less for arranging the music of other composers. The move to Warners initiated a change in working practice, from directing a music department team to operating alone with the help of an orchestrator, enabling him to compose dedicated scores carefully tailored to the narrative demands of each individual film rather than overseeing the collation of short segments of music.

The studio system created enormous pressure on composers, who were contracted to work on large numbers of projects per year by the studio. Steiner's relationship with the head of the music department, Leo Forbstein, was central to the management of this pressure: Forbstein coaxed 13 films in 12 years from Erich Wolfgang Korngold, compared with Steiner's 55 in the same period. Steiner's ability to fulfil the demands placed on him was largely founded in the reliability of his relationship with his chief orchestrator, Hugo Friedhofer: a discussion of the nature of this collaboration follows in the next chapter. In a letter written in 1940, Steiner explains how the pressure on the composer manifests itself, despite the best organisation:

The prospective film composer should be in good physical condition, as we musicians are always the last people to get the picture and almost constantly have to work under terrific pressure. Many times I have to work two days and two nights in succession without an hour's sleep. The reason for this is that pictures are sold in advance and if thru any fault of the studio, delays occur, such as changes in the script, illness of the players, and numerable unforeseen "accidents," the picture still has to be completed and ready to start on its engagement on the day scheduled, so the only thing to do in this case is to work day and night to get it out. I wrote and recorded "We Are Not Alone," which has a continuous score of one hour and ten minutes, in six days. During these six days, I slept eighteen hours at the most. This is a terrific strain on the eyes and the heart, so I would not advise anyone who is not in good physical condition to undertake this vocation, especially as this pressure occurs almost constantly.[47]

The length of Steiner's career and the enormous number of films he scored are noted by almost every biographer and historian: between 1930 and 1963 he wrote music for over 300 films, and he received at least one Oscar nomination every year between 1938 and 1955, except for 1951 and 1953. Although he worked principally for Warner Brothers after 1936, all the major studios, as well as independents such as David Selznick, called on his talents. Nor were the projects minor: for his first twenty years at Warner Brothers, Steiner scored almost exclusively big films with prominent actors and actresses in the cast. He scored many of Errol Flynn's westerns, 19 of Bette Davis's 29 films between 1936 and 1949, and films starring Humphrey Bogart, Gary Cooper, Barbara Stanwyck, Paul Muni, Edward G. Robinson, Cary Grant and James Cagney. He also scored many films which are landmarks for non-musical reasons: *Gone with the Wind* (1939) and *Casablanca* (1943) were both extremely successful at the Oscars; *Mildred Pierce* (1945) brought an Oscar for Joan Crawford; *The Big Sleep* (1946) and *The Treasure of the Sierra Madre* (1948), two films which define Bogart's career; the controversial *Johnny Belinda* (1948). It would be surprising if the pressure to deliver at a continually high level did not show in his work, and the most obvious manifestation occurs in the occasional repetition of material. The volume of music required for the westerns of the 1930s and 1940s demanded considerable time and effort just to notate what were frequently frantic passages of sequential semiquaver motifs: for example, for *They Died with Their Boots On* (1942), Steiner borrowed a military fanfare motif from his score for *Santa Fe Trail* (1940), large segments of vigorous string and bugle texture from *Virginia City* (1940), music to accompany a brawl from *Gold Is Where You Find It* (1938), and a brief *agitato* from *Dodge City* (1939) . He also reused melodic material, perhaps most notably in the recycling of the love theme from *Now, Voyager* as the love theme in *Mildred Pierce* (1945).

Tony Thomas suggests that with Steiner's death from cancer in December 1971 "a link with Old Vienna ceased to be and yet another door on the Old Hollywood was closed". However, the connection with past glories was already breaking during the 1950s.[48] As trends in film scoring changed, absorbing more of the contemporary popular idiom than had been the case in the 1930s and 1940s, it seems increasingly unusual that Steiner continued to be employed to write in his particular tonal orchestral idiom when both jazz and dissonant styles were emerging through the film scores of composers such as Bernard Herrmann, Miklos Rosza and Elmer Bernstein. Steiner's style of scoring was ultimately defined as much by his initial design for scoring practice in the formative 1930s as it was by the idiom of his theatrical background: he may have become trapped by his own success, unable to develop any contrasting practices because his original style remained usable until it fell out of fashion.

So, although Steiner had continued to compose for Hollywood long after the decline of the studio system, a system in which he had functioned most effectively, his place in the chronology of film music is most clearly seen as being at the beginning. His first career in theatre became an apprenticeship for his second in cinema: the easy juxtaposition of verbal/visual narratives and music gave him many models with which to understand music's dramatic potential, and his engagement with European and American popular styles gave him a medium in which to make this understanding accessible to the audience. The conception of music as an extension of the existing narrative seems to have been extremely logical to Steiner: giving every character a theme equates to giving them a song or an aria, a voice with which to express themselves and their emotions. While directors and producers fretted over the disruption caused by music in such a verbally driven narrative, Steiner saw an existing connection in musical theatre, its stretches of speech and dialogue providing a closer relationship with film than opera. Hollywood scoring gave him a chance to stay with what he knew, developing a language of film scoring from his theatrical vocabulary of melody and dramatic gesture yet without the confinements of fitting a melody to a lyric. Music could speak in its language of emotions and expressions, and though he found his approach restricted in other ways, Steiner found the logical heir to musical theatre in film.

———— Chapter 2 ————

STEINER'S TECHNIQUE
OF FILM SCORING

As principal composer on a film, Steiner himself took responsibility for developing all the thematic material and designing the orchestration. Given the pressure of time, however, which increasingly affected music departments during the boom in output from Hollywood in the 1940s, it was usual to find co-composers and orchestrators working with the principal composer. Many of his scores in the late 1930s and early 1940s were orchestrated by Hugo Friedhofer, who rose to prominence as a principal composer himself during the late 1940s.[1] Friedhofer had the responsibility of translating Steiner's short four-stave scores into complete sets of parts for the instruments in the orchestra, and he was also expected to create or copy accompaniment textures for the melodic outlines sketched into the short score by the composer. The scores are full of annotations and messages from composer to orchestrator, and Steiner was always generous in his appreciation of Friedhofer's ability to interpret his ideas and particularly his attention to the use of instruments to create specific textures. This level of communication was extremely advantageous both to Steiner, who could have confidence in his orchestrator's ability, and to the smooth running of the post-production system, for farming out part of the process to others was more likely to get the job done quickly than relying on one composer. Steiner and Erich Wolfgang Korngold both used Friedhofer as their orchestrator for Warner Brothers scores in the late 1930s and early 1940s. Though their music is different in structure and narrative function, both composers created detailed and colourful instrumental textures, and Friedhofer's own original scores of the late 1940s share this common quality of rich and beautifully crafted orchestration.

Figure 2.1: First Page of Max Steiner's short score for *Now, Voyager.*

Source: Now, Voyager. © M. Witmark & Sons, USA. Reproduced by permission of IMP Ltd. Courtesy of Photographic Archives, Harold B. Lee Library, Brigham Young University, Provo, Utah.

THE SCORES

Before addressing the content and function of the scores in more detail, it is interesting to note what a typical Steiner score looks like (see figure 2.1). The scores he wrote, and later kept, of his own work are the original 'short score' versions of the music recorded from which the orchestrators drew up the full orchestral parts. These scores were composed reel by reel, rather than scene by scene: each new musical cue is begun on a fresh sheet of manuscript, as is each new reel, even when a *segue* is required. This is because the music was usually recorded by reel, rather than by scene, so the composer tailored his material to fit the technological demands of the process. Most of the music is written across a system of four staves, or occasionally six when a complex thematic or instrumental texture is required, and there are normally three bars to a stave.[2] Steiner does not assign instruments to individual staves, but the top three staves usually have a treble clef, and the lowest has a bass clef; however, he appears to use the stave system hierarchically to show the function of different instruments in the construction of the musical texture. The top two staves are usually used for melody and countermelody, and the lower two for harmonising parts, often chordal, or for further countermelodic lines or heavily rhythmic lines. He distributes the instruments across the staves, according to the role that they will play in relation to melody or harmony.

The flexibility of the four-stave short score lies in the lack of instrumental attribution in the template. Steiner is able to show the many changes in instrumental detail by appropriate annotation, without the complexity of a full score. This simplifies and hastens the job of the composer and of the conductor, who could use this short score for conducting the recording sessions.[3] For the orchestrator, however, this shorthand is the only hard evidence to use alongside experience of the composer's idiom when the task of orchestrating from the short score to individual instrumental parts begins. The advantage of the extensive and lengthy collaboration between Steiner and Hugo Friedhofer becomes obvious in this context, in that the composer could use shorthand and abbreviations to indicate detail and, once the style for the score had been established, could save further time by simply using the barest melodic outline.

Depending on the material of a score, Steiner often chose not to use a key signature, but to write in accidentals where appropriate. For thematic material that uses sequential modulation or chromaticism, or for music used to build tension by rising chromatic steps or diminished intervals, it seems to have been simpler and quicker for him than working within notated keys.[4] Furthermore, when he restates a thematic idea after its original presentation, he orientates the transposed restatement to the original in terms of the distance by tone, rather than in terms of a new key: "*come sopra*—one tone higher."[5]

The most striking aspect of the written scores is the level of attention to detail. The placement of dynamics, tempo, stylistic markings and phrasings suggests that Steiner had a very precise expectation of how the score would be realised in performance. There is a wealth of annotations to the musical notation, and he used a number of coloured pencils to add different types of detail. Percussion is often added in blue, red, or occasionally green, as a later addition to the basic sketches in dark grey pencil. The impression is that the basic orchestral detail was included while the music was being composed, and that Steiner came back to the scores on subsequent occasions to add other types of detail: such additions would usually be emphatic reminders to the orchestrator or suggestions of alternatives thought up in retrospect. Steiner often makes a feature of extra percussion or non-standard instrumentation such as celeste, vibraphone, melodia, novachord, finger cymbal or side drum. He also developed a few extra emphatic expression markings: "Pomposo," "Screwissimmo," "Schmalzando," "Tragico" and "Mysterioissimmo." Above all, this vast conception of detail demonstrates faith in the chain of communication from composer to finished product.

In some scores, Steiner needed to create music that was to be heard diegetically by an on-screen ensemble, or he needed to match diegetic timbres in the non-diegetic score. In these cases, he would often provide extremely detailed lists of instruments to be used, drawing on his experience and knowledge of theatre and marching bands. For example, a diegetic band in *The Adventures of Mark Twain* (1944) is described as follows: "[o]rchestrate like small town band in picture—2 fl + picc, 2 cl, 2 trpts, 2 Horns, 1 TRB, Tuba."[6] Later in the same film he wants to create the sound of a nineteenth-century salon orchestra, asking for: "4 violins, 2nd, 1 Viola, 1 Cello, 1 Bas, 1 fl, 1 Clar, Piano, Harp."[7] Similarly, his feel for the dramatic power of the music can be seen in the extensive margin notes that he wrote to himself and to the orchestrator and conductor in the scores, in order to emphasise what he was thinking as he wrote the music. Some of these are purely descriptive; for example, this note for a scene between Charlotte and Tina in *Now, Voyager* indicates how the music is to be felt: "INTENSE not fast (a child pleading) not bleeding."[8] In *The Oklahoma Kid* (1939), Steiner makes stylistic reference to an earlier age to describe the theme for the female love interest: "Mozart-ish: (The girl's theme (strings, harps, celeste, flute, vibraph))."[9] Similarly in *They Died with Their Boots On* (1942), he describes a dramatic moment of music for a scene as resembling "A Warner Bros.—"Tosca" at the end—verstehst!"[10] The score for *In This Our Life* (1941) seems to have particularly inspired Steiner. As the central protagonist, Stanley Timberlake, flirts with her elderly uncle to gain his help in buying her off a drunk-driving charge, Steiner describes the music as "Eine Kleine "Incest" musik."[11] He accompanies a sequence leading to the character plunging fatally off a cliff with the thoughts: "The Police Car (Thank God). Hugo! Orchestrated full BUT played pp (misterioso) gong, vibra, pianos etc.!! The "Law" will get the BITCH! goody-goody."[12] Similarly, in *Mildred Pierce*, he couples his feelings for one of the characters with a specific choice of instrumentation: "screwy, Hugo! as "NASTY" AS POSSIBLE—(w.w. only??)"[13]

The scores also include margin notes that are not fundamental to the interpretation or orchestration of the short score but which give an indication of Steiner's attitude to his work and reveal something of his true nature. Sometimes, the pressure of work shows: during only the second cue of *Now,*

Voyager, he seems frustrated by the demands of orchestration: "swimmy—VIBRA??? (I'm sick of VIBRAPHONE.)"[14] In *Dodge City* (1939) he annotates a trivial line of dialogue which begins "How d'you like these here onions?" with the thought: "God help us!—The whole picture is like that—I am resigning!"[15] In *They Died with Their Boots On,* Steiner is underscoring a formal meeting between the film's two lovers, but his thoughts on the way music should be used have clearly been overtaken by the ideas of the director, Raoul Walsh. Halfway through the cue, Steiner notes: "Music stops—if it were *my* picture."[16] His comments can also be crude, focusing on implications of sexual attraction and romance in the films. Many of these are quite blunt, particularly in the score for the Errol Flynn film *Dodge City*, but the tone of the comments is usually harmless. In *Now, Voyager*, beside the first love scene, Steiner is quite understated, noting: "Erwachende Liebe!! Verstehst? or SEX rears its ugly head!"[17]

It is through the scores as documents that Steiner is most clearly seen: witty, versatile, shrewd, lewd, completely conversant with his environment and the social and political dynamics of the studio, alert to the ironies and truths of the characterisations he was expressing, a confident communicator who drew on a wide orchestral and cultural vocabulary in the creation of his music. Despite the fact that he must often have been exhausted while composing, and that he was clearly uninspired by some of the material that he was interpreting, the most striking feature of the scores is the enormous energy which they convey. The flamboyance of the notation, with copious underlining, long sweeping slurs, the thickness of note beams, the string, harp and piano glissandi in different colours, reflects in the written score much of the animation it would feature in performance. The sense of the score, however, is easily gathered at a glance, and the notation is rarely indecipherable.

THE METHODS OF SCORING

Almost all Steiner's scores were composed in post-production from a rough cut of the film. Frequently, this cut would change during the director's editing process, making life complicated for the composer and orchestrator: Steiner and David Selznick fell out over the director's constant re-editing of *Gone with the Wind* (1939), as Selznick believed that the composers should be able to work with a rough cut which might change. The addition of music in post-production gives the composer the advantage of interpreting the film from much the same position as an audience might receive it: Steiner noted that he usually watched the film alone for the first viewing, but that the director came in at a later stage "if he so desire[d]."[18] This position, as expressed in the autobiography, is probably coloured a little by memory: it is unlikely that Steiner would have been allowed such independence of thought and interpretation. Directors and producers such as Michael Curtiz and Jack Warner usually wanted to be involved at this stage: letters from David Selznick to Steiner certainly indicate that the two men shared a view on how a score might be structured. Hal B. Wallis, who produced both *Now, Voyager* and *Casablanca* was also interested in the music: Aljean Harmetz notes that it was common for Wallis to provide many pages of detailed and well informed notes for Steiner and Korngold regarding the orchestration and placement of music.[19]

Steiner goes on to describe being inspired to write "a few tunes or themes," which in many scores is an understatement, for his melodic invention is often extremely expansive. Kathryn Kalinak notes his clear emphasis on that element of technique in his discussion of the score for *The Informer* (1935), about which he remarks "[e]very character should have a theme."[20] Much later in his life, in an interview with Tony Thomas near the end of his career, Steiner was enthusiastic, but vague about his technique:

There is no method. Some pictures require a lot of music, and some are so realistic that music would only interfere. Most of my films were entertainments—soap operas, story book adventures, fantasies. If those films were made today, they would be made differently and I would score them differently. But my attitude would be the same—to give the film what it needs. And with me, if the picture is good, the score stands a better chance of being good.[21]

There is a certain element of contradiction here: it suggests that he was not a man to analyse his own methods, and when invited to do so, he found many different ways to explain his work that did not necessarily complement each other. The following overview of Steiner's technique of composition brings out the main elements to be found in any of his scores and provides a framework within which one is able to appreciate the structure of the score for *Now, Voyager*.

Thematic Material as Characterisation

Virtually any score by Steiner is dominated by the manipulation of thematic material, both original and pre-composed, but always with a strong emphasis on melodic effect. The trend in the scores for using themes to emphasise character portrayal is a likely consequence of the emphasis on the star system prevalent in film-making in this period. Further, genres that emphasise the drama of relationships, rather than action, clearly invite the audience to focus on the personalities of the plot. Many of the films he scored fall into that category, particularly the 'women's' films and the biographical pictures of historical figures.

The level of thematic characterisation is influenced by broad generic factors as well as specific storyline details. For example, *The Oklahoma Kid* (1939), a comedy Western vehicle for James Cagney, is based on a strong moral discourse about right and wrong, a balance typical of the Western genre. Cagney's role is that of a man perceived as an outlaw, who appears to oppose the code of law represented by the town sheriff. Steiner creates a strong diatonic triad-based theme for the law-abiding townsfolk, epitomised by the sheriff's family, and a quirky chromatic motif for Cagney's eponymous hero. The contrast of diatonic and chromatic language evokes a basic contrast in musical idioms, but it also epitomises the fundamental right/wrong or normal/other discourse of the Western.

Figure 2.2a: Max Steiner, Main Title theme
The Oklahoma Kid **(1939) score, p. 2.**
Source: The Oklahoma Kid. © W.B. Music Corp., USA. Reproduced by
permission of IMP Ltd.

Figure 2.2b: Max Steiner, The Kid's theme
The Oklahoma Kid **score, pp. 14-15.**
Source: The Oklahoma Kid. © W.B. Music Corp., USA. Reproduced by
permission of IMP Ltd.

In the score for *The Gay Sisters* (1942) Steiner uses a similar contrast, but within one theme rather than two: the Gaylord sisters, whose lives the film follows, have a proud, military melody which evokes their sense of family identity, but in responding to the devious actions of the middle sister, Evelyn, Steiner introduces dissonance and woodwind instrumentation to reinvent the theme specifically for her. The basic contrast between diatonic and chromatic language can be used as a standard for characteristic interpretation. Diatonic writing, particularly in major tonalities, becomes associated with happiness, honour, strength, valour, mainstream values of right rather than wrong. Chromaticism becomes associated with quirkiness, the unusual, personalities at odds with the norm, wrong rather than right, unhappiness, and dissonance with the environment in which the characters find themselves.[22] The score for *They Died with Their Boots On* (1942) uses this scheme to characterise a double opposition between central character George Armstrong Custer and his two distinct enemies, Lieutenant Sharp and the Sioux tribe. While Custer's theme is a simple diatonic design, both 'enemies' are characterised musically with chromatic themes. The difference between Custer's blunt openness and Sharp's deviousness is captured in the difference between the large open intervals of the former theme and the stepwise motion of the latter. However, the military backgrounds of both men are symbolised in the dotted rhythms of both themes, giving them something in common musically, despite the differing characteristics. This attention to the detail of a theme works well for a film with strong individual characters rather than a broad generic story type.

Figure 2.3a: Max Steiner, Custer's theme
***They Died with Their Boots On* (1942) score, p. 16.**
Source: They Died with Their Boots On. © W.B. Music Corp., USA. Reproduced by permission of IMP Ltd.

Figure 2.3b: Max Steiner, Sharp's theme
***They Died with Their Boots On* score, p. 18.**
Source: They Died with Their Boots On. © W.B. Music Corp., USA. Reproduced by permission of IMP Ltd.

Melodramatic plots often displayed a range of intensity and character development which was well suited to Steiner's carefully crafted characterisation in music. *Mildred Pierce* (1945), for example, features two strong female characters and two weaker male characters in a plot of emotional conflict and dramatic developments. As *film noir*, Steiner has aimed for a less sentimental approach than in other films about women, such as *The Gay Sisters*, producing a more complex range of themes to evoke the varied characters. Mildred Pierce is a determined woman, and her theme is strident, using triadic movement and sudden changes of direction. By contrast the theme for Mildred's daughters, Veda and Kay, is simple and scalic, reflecting Mildred's initial perception of them as children. This contrasts with the claustrophobia of the simple repetitively intense theme to represent the inert marriage between Mildred and her first husband Bert.

Figure 2.4a: Max Steiner, Mildred's theme
Mildred Pierce **(1945) score, pp. 2-4.**
Source: Mildred Pierce. © M. Witmark & Sons, USA. Reproduced by
permission of IMP Ltd.

Figure 2.4b: Max Steiner, Veda and Kay's theme
Mildred Pierce **score, pp. 37-39.**
Source: Mildred Pierce. © M. Witmark & Sons, USA. Reproduced by
permission of IMP Ltd.

Figure 2.4c: Max Steiner, Mildred and Bert's theme
Mildred Pierce **score, pp. 35-36.**
Source: Mildred Pierce. © M. Witmark & Sons, USA. Reproduced by
permission of IMP Ltd.

This scheme of thematic material differs from the more obvious binary
opposition of diatonic and chromatic writing. Steiner has tried to capture the
detail of the characters, creating themes which are all essentially tonal, but whose
compass, melodic design, rhythm and connotation imply more complex

distinctions between characters. The childish simplicity of the daughters' theme uses stepwise motion in contrast with the passionate sweeping of Mildred's theme, but Steiner brings out the sinister undertone of daughter Veda with clarinet and woodwind instrumentation instead of 'purer' strings. Arguably, this type of thematic detail would not have impressed itself on the audience in the way that it can be analysed objectively. Instrumental distinctions and the fundamentally different moods of diatonic and chromatic writing are probably the limit of a spectator/listener's auditory appreciation while watching a film. Steiner does not, however, seem to be deterred from providing the musical clues and interpretations even though his audience may not be completely aware of them. His use of melody to give musical characterisation a striking definition is a distinctive feature of the Steiner technique, and it gives every score a sense of intellectual interpretation as well as atmospheric reaction.

Steiner's themes also employ musical stereotypes in forming their characteristic impressions. The march and the waltz feature particularly frequently in the themes he wrote, stylistic references that are rooted in the late nineteenth- and early twentieth-century musical theatre styles of his background. The main themes from *The Oklahoma Kid*, *The Gay Sisters* and *Desperate Journey* (1942) all employ the strong four beat pulse and dotted rhythms of the military style. These features also characterise the themes of strong characters within more complex melodic schemes: Mildred Pierce, Mrs Vale in *Now, Voyager* and Custer in *They Died with Their Boots On*.

The waltz style has romantic connotations, which Steiner duly exploits, but not without a sense of irony or a perverse reinterpretation of the basic elements. In the score for *In This Our Life* (1942), Steiner uses chromaticism and rhythm to reinvent the waltz idea for the different characterisations. For Bette Davis's selfish vamp, Stanley, he borrows symbolically, though not literally, from the dance music Stanley listens to for escape from her troubles. The angularity of the chromatic motif contrasts with the stepwise simplicity of the theme for her decent, long-suffering sister Roy (Olivia de Havilland). Roy's theme has its own complexity though, creating a three beat feel against a four beat metre.

Figure 2.5a: Max Steiner, Stanley's theme
***In This Our Life* (1942) score, p. 21.**
Source: In This Our Life. © M. Witmark & Sons, USA. Reproduced by
permission of IMP Ltd.

Figure 2.5b: Max Steiner, Roy's theme
***In This Our Life* score, p. 6.**
Source: In This Our Life. © M. Witmark & Sons, USA. Reproduced by
permission of IMP Ltd.

Steiner also uses the waltz ironically in *Dark Victory*, to evoke the tragedy
of the heroine's tranquil equanimity with death. Here the chromaticism brings
unease to a melody which, without the extra accidentals, would be sad but not
ominous.

Figure 2.6: Max Steiner, Death theme
***Dark Victory* (1939) score, pp. 92-93.**
Source: Dark Victory. © Remick M Corp., USA. Reproduced by
permission of IMP Ltd.

Steiner occasionally uses pre-composed music as thematic material in his
scores, usually when their involvement is prescribed by action in the script. In
The Great Lie (1941) Steiner uses the principal melody of the opening movement
of Tchaikovsky's First Piano Concerto to capture the dramatic personality of
Mary Astor's concert pianist. The non-diegetic use of the melody separates her
glamorous independence from the homely aspirations of the other characters, so
that the score perpetuates the character's concealment of her true feelings. In *We
Are Not Alone* (1939) he uses the theme from Haydn's "Surprise" Symphony, to
represent the innocence, both literal and legal, of the character who plays it on
his violin.[23] Perhaps the most famous example is the use of the popular song "As
Time Goes By" in the score for *Casablanca* (1943). Although he is said to have
been unhappy about having to use the song so extensively, Steiner created a
dramatic score that retained the distinctive memorability of the song's melody in
rich and complex non-diegetic writing. Furthermore, he used "La Marseillaise"
and "Deutschland über alles" to provide the basis for much of the remainder of
the thematic expression in the non-diegetic music, designing an original score
from pre-composed melodic material.[24]

The range of application of thematic characterisation in Steiner's scores of this period is enormous. He was able to create thematic constructions with a complexity of design and conception which, though they relied on essentially simple musical contrasts and ideas such as chromaticism, waltz rhythms, or orchestration, reflected the complexity of the film texts. He knew the limitations of thematic design in the interpretative faculty of his average audience, yet he did not allow that to restrict the flow of his imagination and the formalisation of the response in the creation of the score. He was, however, equally capable of creating simple scores that focused more generally on atmosphere, under-emphasised complexities of characterisation, or, indeed, that seemed not to have fired his creativity at all.

Pre-composed Music

There are two reasons for the inclusion of pre-composed music in the original non-diegetic scores composed by Steiner. One is that a piece of music has been used in the action and that he has been advised to use it in the score or has felt that its significance to the plot would serve the score well. The other is to provide authenticity to the score by using music appropriate to a particular period or locale to emphasise the action indirectly. The former case is not one which he was comfortable with: "Never use music which people have heard before and which may detract from the action of the picture. . . . by the time they [have] finished arguing about the music they [do not] know what the picture [is] all about."[25]

Steiner's choice of pre-composed material for authentic purposes adds intellectual fluency to scores of all types, regardless of the arrangement of original material. Authenticity usually required him to use national anthems or partisan melodies, although exceptions include Mendelssohn's "Wedding March" and nursery rhymes. A striking example is the title sequence to *Desperate Journey*, which uses "Wacht am Rhein," harmonised in the minor, leading into "Rule Britannia." The film's titles are superimposed over a montage linking a map of Germany into the film's first action, and to use an original theme composed to represent the Allies here would have complicated the clear visual references of the opening sequence.

The sheer length of *Gone with the Wind* invited more melodic material than Steiner might have felt could be developed through thematic characterisation, and the large quantity of quotation from popular songs of the period in the non-diegetic score is a testament to this. Steiner drew from songs by composers such as Stephen Collins Foster, including "Beautiful Dreamer" and "The Old Folks at Home," as well as from other melodies with military connotations, such as "Marching through Georgia," "Bonnie Blue Flag" and "Cavaliers of Dixie." Such melodic colour reflects the detail of the film visually and dramatically and suggests that Steiner's richest scores were written for films that inspired him in this way. Similarly, he uses many Confederate and Union songs to amplify the central conflict of the partisan struggle in *Virginia City* (1940), which compensates for the simple thematic content of the score. Some of his motivation for this score was probably drawn from Miriam Hopkins's role as a Confederate spy pretending to be a bar-room singer entertaining the Union troops. The duplicity of her character is partly established through her diegetic performance of the songs, and Steiner draws on these connotations in the non-diegetic score. He would have been obliged to use certain songs because they were included in the script. This is certainly the case in *Virginia City* and *They Died with Their Boots On*: the latter film employs the real life anthem of Custer's Seventh Cavalry, the Irish folk song "Garryowen" in the narrative, and Steiner draws on the diegetic statements for some non-diegetic scoring of battle sequences involving the regiment.

Discussion of pre-composed music in a film is sometimes hampered in that the scores do not always provide evidence of who was responsible for the choice of music. The final shooting script for *Mildred Pierce* does not note the specific music in three instances of public domain music, so it is possible that Steiner made the selection himself. Certainly the music to accompany Monte Beragon's seduction of Mildred is an ironic delight: Beragon puts on a gramophone record, a slow jazz band version of "It Can't Be Wrong," the lyricised song version of the love theme from *Now, Voyager*.[26]

Given the diversity of films Steiner scored, the variety of pre-composed material he referred to is relatively narrow. This is due in part to the limitations placed on him by the genres of films he was composing for. The Civil War setting of the large number of Westerns would have provided a wide choice of melodies, yet to make a clear melodic description of the two sides in the war, Steiner limited himself in many scores to "The Battle Hymn of the Republic," "Dixie" and "Yankee Doodle Dandy." Similarly, when wartime stories required indication of national or partisan allegiance national anthems were repeatedly used.

Orchestration

Steiner's attention to orchestral detail is apparent when looking at the scores, but the extent to which the detail is heard is rather more difficult to ascertain. Different instrumental groupings certainly play a prominent role in sustaining the authentic atmosphere of period public domain music and in the strength of character definitions. In the former case, the instruments are often part of the diegetic soundtrack, such as the saloon piano or military bugle, although many of the Westerns he scored bring the bugle into the non-diegetic score.[27]

In *The Great Lie*, Steiner uses instrumentation as part of character definition, although the gesture here is not one of his most subtle. He identifies Mary Astor's concert pianist in the non-diegetic parts of the score with the inclusion of piano or with imitation of the original orchestral texture which accompanies her grand concert performances in the early part of the film. He is more subtle and versatile in the score for *Mildred Pierce*, where he represents Mildred's experiences of honesty and manipulation with contrasting instrumentations. Mildred's elder daughter, Veda, has aspirations to wealth and society far beyond her mother's means, as does Mildred's lover, Monte. Steiner consistently represents the 'otherness' of this existence with jazz and woodwind instrumentation and constructs an instrumental connection between Veda and Monte long before their real relationship begins. The chromatic blues clarinet version of Veda's theme refers to the jazz idiom with all its sophisticated connotations and supports Veda's upwardly mobile desires, as manifested in her 'alternative' career as a cabaret artiste and her mature attitude to her own sexuality. The instrumentation also suggests that Veda's perception of herself is similar to Mildred's perception of Monte: glamorous, sexy, sophisticated, far removed from her (Mildred's and Veda's) own reality. By contrast, the simplicity and blandness of Mildred's relatively poor married lifestyle is recreated musically with strings, as in her own theme, which is dominated by a rich string texture.

The binary opposition of strings and woodwind is created in the context of an orchestral style generally dominated by stringed instruments. Steiner frequently used the string section of the orchestra to carry the main melodic material of the score, usually employing a broad dynamic range and pitch compass to create a rich texture. It is this which has led critics to describe his writing as symphonic, referring to the string-led idioms of nineteenth-century European symphonic writing.[28] Certainly he uses the full orchestra for expressive purposes, and his juxtaposition of timbres of different instruments and orchestral sections does bear comparison with the idiom of Tchaikovsky, for example. However, as Steiner's comments recorded in the last chapter indicate, his orchestration design was drawn from an economic imperative to create variety from as few instruments as possible. The expansive formal design of the nineteenth century symphony provided a context for the development of orchestral texture, but a film score requires an immediate effect in a compact delivery. From the earliest of his film scores, there is a scheme of orchestration based on fundamental contrasts between high pitches and low, sonorous and reedy tones, strings, wind and brass. These contrasts, coupled with dynamic, harmonic and melodic features, can reflect emotional qualities as well as provide a functional formula that is economically practical for studio purposes.

In Steiner's music, stringed instruments seem to function as the 'norm' because of their prevalence in the orchestration. The string family—violins, violas, 'cellos and double basses—provides a timbral unity, even when simultaneously carrying different melodic lines, which gives much greater flexibility to scoring than any other family of the orchestra. Furthermore, the ability to encompass a huge range of pitch within this single timbre makes melodic statements very striking: many of his main title cues employ this approach. Against such a strong sound, woodwind instruments are less effective, so he often used brass, particularly horns, for counter melodies and contrasts. He was also concerned with the relative pitching of instruments and actors' voices, and he made careful choices of instrumentation to support dialogue. This also sometimes ruled out woodwind as an option because of the similar timbres.

When I write my music I try to keep away from the pitch [of the different actors' voices] because when the picture is dubbed, if the music is kept low and is in the same register as the talk, it is lost. If the music is loud, the director may complain that it interferes with the dialogue and ask me to hold it down. . . . If the voice is low I write some high register music. If the speaking voice is high, I write in low register. . . . It isn't always easy to write this way because a man with a bass voice usually has a very dramatic part and how are you going to get drama out with high violins? That is another story, but it is my secret.[29]

Just as Steiner has used chromaticism to represent otherness in thematic design, so woodwind and brass instruments take on similar associations. This is given even greater significance by the limited potential for woodwind in combination with strings. For timbral, as well as dramatic reasons, he appears to have found woodwind more useful as a section on their own in developing material: both the Sioux theme and Sharp's theme in *They Died with Their Boots On* use distinctive oboe and piccolo instrumentation to separate the themes further from the unison string version of Custer's theme. The motif for James Cagney's outlaw, the Oklahoma Kid, is also orchestrated for oboe, the reedy quality adding a certain quirkiness to the characterisation. As Rick sees Ilsa for the first time in his *Casablanca* cafe, non-diegetic woodwind instruments make a striking entry into the silent void after Sam stops playing the piano. The sedate but yearning oboe version of what is obviously 'their' song speaks for their exchange of looks.

Steiner clearly saw orchestration as a key part in a successful score. He continually sought exactly the right balance between melody and accompaniment, down to specifying the number of violins required. He also used a wide range of instruments, including ocarina,[30] banjo,[31] Hammond organ,[32] novachord,[33] melodia[34] and finger cymbal.[35] Despite a score-writing technique which often seems to be little more than a sketch through repetition of thematic material, Steiner still sought as much variety in the way material was expressed as in what it was expressing.

Physical Action and Comedy

The placement of music in response to physical actions on the screen is the area of scoring practice for which Steiner has been most criticised. His apparent penchant for catching every movement seen on screen has been interpreted in more recent, sophisticated contexts as trivialising the narrative function of music: Claudia Gorbman describes it as "hyperexplicit"; Kathryn Kalinak suggests that Steiner "exploit[s] each and every opportunity for music [giving it a] hyperbolic quality."[36] It is important however, to draw a distinction between occasions when music imitates or mimics physical action as a means of providing insight into the experiences of the characters, and situations where the mickey-mousing is placed for uncomplicated emphatic effect. The former case occurs in some of Steiner's early scores: for *Of Human Bondage* (1934), he uses a combination of uneven rhythm and dissonant chords to capture the physical and social discomfort of Philip Carey's limp. It appears to be a simple imitation of the rhythm in which the character walks, yet the harmonic effects create a strong sense of how Carey views his own disfigurement. Similarly, in the score for *The Informer* (1935) the well-chronicled catching of the dripping water in Gypo Nolan's cell uses the imitation of action to emphasise the anxiety that the character is feeling.

During the late 1930s and early 1940s Steiner was given an increasing number of Westerns and wartime films to score. Both of these genres include lengthy fight or chase sequences, with limited dialogue and fast-paced editing, which provides a different challenge from for example, the character-driven, slower pace of melodramatic genres. Scores for action pictures often used a very simple structure of two or three themes, while much of the rest of the music was used to provide coherence to the fight or action montages. In these sequences Steiner employed the mickey-mousing of both partisan allegiance and the cut and thrust of physical gesture, often creating busy cues running for many pages at a time. The extent of his scoring of action sequences can be seen clearly in the sheer length of some of the scores for action genres: *Santa Fe Trail,* 309 pages; *They Died with Their Boots On*, 317 pages; *Desperate Journey*, 222 pages. By contrast, melodramas such as *Mildred Pierce* at 154 pages and *The Great Lie* at 189 pages, are significantly shorter, despite the films being of a comparable length at between 105 and 120 minutes. Steiner's repertoire for capturing physical actions in these films is frequently limited to short, rhythmic motifs. He describes the second example here, where the hero leaps onto a runaway team of horses, as "Walkyrie like."

Figure 2.7: Max Steiner, Galloping Horse motif
***The Oklahoma Kid* score, p. 18.**
Source: The Oklahoma Kid. © W.B. Music Corp., USA. Reproduced by
permission of IMP Ltd.

Figure 2.8: Max Steiner, Walkyrie motif *Dodge City* (1939) score, p. 89.
Source: Dodge City. © M. Witmark & Sons, USA. Reproduced by
permission of IMP Ltd.

Above all, writing music for battle sequences was dominated by two factors: the length of time it took to write music dominated by fast rhythms such as semiquavers, and the potential inaudibility of the finished product when mixed with the sound effects track. For *They Died with Their Boots On* (1942), which includes the epic Battle of the Little Big Horn, Steiner lifted some of his own music for the battle sequences from the score of *Santa Fe Trail* (1940), a film that also featured General Custer. Justification for such economy of effort can be found in his comments to a newspaper about the scoring of *Santa Fe Trail*: "It takes eight thousand notes for Errol Flynn to kill a man. . . . He killed thousand and thousands of men and I wrote millions and millions of notes."[37]

The problem of audibility is clear in the scores for *Desperate Journey* and *Captains of the Clouds*, where the diegetic aircraft noise prevents a large range of the orchestral timbre from being heard. Steiner sought to overcome inaudibility with shorter, more consciously audible musical gestures, and many of these can be identified as the simplistic type of mickey-mousing. In *Desperate Journey*, for example, he captures the spitting of peppercorns by a character with a shrill piccolo glissando, which cuts through the domination of the diegetic soundscape by aircraft engines. He uses the device a number of times in the scene, which becomes repetitive although it is an effective use of music in a limited context. He viewed this type of mimicry as humorous, or at least potentially so, but the scores suggest that he was not comfortable with using music in this way. For *The Adventures of Mark Twain* director Jesse Lasky made many suggestions to Steiner about how to bring the visual comedy across in the music, but the composer's explanation of each comic moment in the score margin shows that such interpretation was not automatic to him. He explains his intentions to Friedhofer for these moments in ways that he would not usually use for themes or melodic moments: when a group of cadets trip and fall in *They Died with Their Boots On*, Steiner writes "Cb against C# intentional . . . supposedly funny."[38]

In this context, Steiner seems to have regarded the catching of certain physical gestures as a necessary part of the job. The limited comedy of *Now, Voyager* is focused in the mountain excursion scene, which reaches its first climax in the car accident. The music which accompanies the journey up the mountain captures both Jerry and Charlotte's increasing uncertainty about their driver and journey and the building romantic tension between them. The hysteria of the plunge over the cliff edge is rather underplayed in the score: Steiner chooses to accompany the reversing of the car, but carefully places only a low sforzando chord, which is faded low in volume, under the actual crash of the car.[39]

There are strong consistencies in scoring technique across many of the films of this period, particularly in the combination of thematic characterisation and striking instrumentation. However, the employment of these features remains flexible to the demands of the film's structure and genre, and elements of Steiner's technique can be organised into generic responses. The consistency of approach can also be attributed to the high rate of composition of scores, particularly between 1936 and 1945, which required a consolidation of practices and processes used by both Steiner and his orchestrators. The 1940s' scores do not show the ingenuity of the previous decade's work, but they do demonstrate how Steiner continued to be creative in the employment of his tried and tested techniques. In this context, the Academy Award for *Now, Voyager* epitomises this fusion of creativity and technical coherence and is a tribute to his contribution to film composition as much as to the individual achievement of this score.

Chapter 3

HISTORICAL AND CRITICAL CONTEXT OF *NOW, VOYAGER*

CONTEXT OF PRODUCTION

Warner Brothers

The content of films produced at Warner Brothers evolved enormously during the period between the coming of sound and the end of the Second World War, initially in response to a consolidation of the production process and later in reaction to the changing social context of wartime America. The depression of the late 1920s and early 1930s caused the studio to restructure itself financially and industrially, creating what Thomas Schatz describes as "a ruthlessly cost-efficient, factory-oriented mass-production mentality. That meant tighter budgets on all features, a more streamlined studio operation . . . and a highly formulaic and routinized approach to its films and filmmaking."[1] During the pre-war era, Warners relied on a few generic formulae which were often tied to particular star artists; however competition and the defection of a few key figures in their operation forced them to adapt to the changing market, creating variations in genre and using previously untried acting partnerships. Once war seemed inevitable in Europe, they began to capitalise on the conflict as a focus for morale building and entertainment, beginning with the controversy of *Confessions of a Nazi Spy* (1939), a semi-documentary about Nazi espionage and the German-American Bund. They were the first studio before 1940 even to consider the European situation as material for film, and both *Confessions* and the extremely successful *The Fighting 69th* (1940) were significant in influencing a change in Hollywood's attitude toward the war.

The Warner genres also reflected gender differences, treating male and female heroism in different ways. From 1938 to 1940 biographical pictures focusing on the contributions of great men to society were made, including *Dr. Ehrlich's Magic Bullet* and *A Dispatch from Reuter's*; in the same year, other historical pictures found their form in Westerns, such as *Virginia City* and *Santa*

Fe Trail, starring Errol Flynn. In 1941 Warners began to reflect the imminence of war with *Dive Bomber* and *Sergeant York* and the reality of war in 1942 with *Captains of the Clouds* and *Desperate Journey*. The male star formulae were also affected by a combination of circumstances at Warner Brothers in 1942: Edward G. Robinson and James Cagney both left for other studios, Ronald Reagan enlisted for military service, and Errol Flynn's medical condition and two rape charges affected his behaviour and his image.

The 'women's' picture tended to deal with heroism in a more homely manner, and the forms that emerged during the war were contemporary variations on those genres which had emerged during the late 1930s: Thomas Schatz categorises them as maternal dramas, love stories, working-girl stories, Gothic thrillers and bio-pics. Maria LaPlace describes how Hollywood executives in this period researched criteria for bringing women to the cinema: "women favoured female stars over male, and preferred in order of preference, serious dramas, love stories, and musicals. Furthermore, women were said to want 'good character development', and stories with 'human interest'."[2] The war brought an acute emphasis to stories of love, motherhood and work, dealing with both the immediacy of the home front—Claudette Colbert was the wife-left-at-home in *Since You Went Away* (1944)—or the stronger international morals of *Watch on the Rhine* (1943), in which Bette Davis played the wife of an Austrian underground leader. Other films ignored the war directly, but showed its influence in other ways: *Now, Voyager* ultimately considers the prospect of bringing up a child without a husband, and *Mildred Pierce* (1945) explores how women survive with only other women to rely on. In any form, Warners' female genres became increasingly successful, partly in response to the high proportion of women in the audience.

Bette Davis

The investment in the woman's film can be seen very clearly in the specific case of Bette Davis, whose casting in *Jezebel* in 1938 initiated the creation of some of Hollywood's most definitive female roles during the first half of the 1940s.

A hit both commercially and critically after its March 1938 release, *Jezebel* [1938] brought Davis another Oscar and solidified Warners' commitment to quality pictures. Suddenly the "female Jimmy Cagney" rap and the urban crime thrillers were behind her, and Davis starred over the next few years in some of the greatest melodramas in Hollywood's history, including *The Sisters* [1938], *Dark Victory* [1939], *The Old Maid* [1939], *All This and Heaven Too* [1940], *The Letter* [1940], *The Great Lie* [1941], *The Little Foxes* [1941] and *Now, Voyager* [1942]. Each of these roles was a variation on the contradictory Julie Marston [Davis's role in *Jezebel*], with Davis cast either as an emasculating shrew or as a charming innocent.[3]

The success of these films encouraged the studio to make more films for women and to expand their portfolio of female stars towards the end of the war, signing Joan Crawford and Barbara Stanwyck on lucrative, high production deals that would last into the latter part of the decade. Power for female actors was established by Davis, however, and as one of the top ten stars during this heyday period in her career, she was a figurehead for consumerist and commercial aspects of film as an entertainment industry. The manipulation of her film image to real life significance formed a central part of the marketing of *Now, Voyager*. LaPlace describes "the promotion of the film as a how-to-be-beautiful guide with Davis as chief instructor."[4] The Pressbook for the film explicitly presents the hair, fashion and beauty aspects of Davis's role as vehicles for the expression of contemporary style.[5]

Richard Dyer explores how Davis's well-publicised independence outside the fictional world, for example in the contractual problems she had with Warners, translated into the independence of her characters on film.[6] She was not alone in this type of transference—Katherine Hepburn and Joan Crawford are other notable examples—but the particular roles Davis played at this time seem to balance the importance of independence with preservation of womanly attributes. In *The Bride Came COD* (1939), a screwball comedy, her evasion of her pilot kidnapper (James Cagney) meets with her attempts to remain beautiful while stuck in an abandoned mining town. In *Dark Victory* (1939) her love of the sporting life and the management of her estate are juxtaposed sharply with the management of the physical symptoms of her brain tumour and her love for the surgeon who prolongs her life. *All This and Heaven Too* (1940) shows Davis as a troubled governess, in a role where she explores the boundaries of her independence in the context of love beyond her station and *in loco parentis* affection. *Now, Voyager* presented her with a chance to show the more vulnerable aspect to her personality: the Pressbook reminds us that Davis came "from New England and therefore knows what an inhibition is."[7]

CRITICAL INTERPRETATIONS OF *NOW, VOYAGER*

In her extensive study of the genre, *A Woman's View*, Jeanine Basinger describes *Now, Voyager* as perhaps "the definitive women's film of all time," as well as one of the most successful and moving.[8] Basinger assesses the women's film as having three main purposes, regardless of the character, plot or setting:

To place a woman at the center of the story universe ("I am a woman, and I am important")
To reaffirm in the end the concept that a woman's true job is that of just being a woman, a job she can't very well escape no matter what else she does, with the repression disguised as *love* ("Love is my true job!")
To provide a temporary visual liberation of some sort, however small—an escape into a purely romantic love, into sexual awareness, into luxury or into the rejection of the female role that might only come in some form of questioning ("What other choices do I have?")
These purposes . . . are at once revealed to be at cross-purposes; they conflict with one another and contradict one another.[9]

Now, Voyager certainly fulfils these narrative and interpretative demands. The film is the story of Charlotte Vale and her own self-conscious evolution towards the recognition of the value of her own role, in the family and in society. Charlotte ultimately accepts the role of mothering Tina Durrance: loving her becomes her job and providing a stable family environment becomes her aim. Charlotte's transition from repressed spinster to independent 'parent' is made possible firstly by her rejection of her mother's control, via the burgeoning passion of her relationship with Jerry, and later on by the intelligent and careful pursuit of independent thought and behaviour, a pursuit which ultimately becomes the rationale for her rejection of her role as Jerry's lover.

However, as Jackie Stacey suggests in her book on Hollywood cinema and its female spectators, the variety of women who watch films, their contexts, the company they keep, and their social and cultural differences "may open up multiple or contradictory readings."[10] For that reason it is virtually impossible to simplify a strategy for reading this film, let alone to consolidate one particular interpretation. *Now, Voyager*'s agenda of independence means something very different to self-sufficient young women in the Western world of the 1990s from the message which would have been received by their grandmothers in 1942. Relationships with mothers and with married men have been affected by changes in social and moral codes, and the contemporary interpretation of the significance of Charlotte's choices is unlikely to match the intentions of Bette Davis, screenwriter Casey Robinson, or director Hal B. Wallis. For that reason, no single reading of the film will be attempted in this chapter; however, in order to make some sense of how Max Steiner experienced the film when creating his score, it is useful to highlight elements of the narrative that define the film's content.

Casey Robinson's screenplay for *Now, Voyager* represents a strategic simplification of the narrative of the original book, *Now, Voyager*, by Olive Higgins Prouty. Prouty's novel relies largely on dialogue to tell the story and to express the experiences of its characters, a narrative method of which Robinson retained significant portions in the screenplay; however, he streamlined Prouty's more extensive use of flashbacks and centralised the concept of the mother-daughter relationship so that it runs throughout the film. In the Treatment, a summary of the novel's potential for filming, Edmund Goulding suggested cutting some of the more minor characters and making the central characters of Charlotte and Jerry much stronger. It would be easy to argue, however, that the film presents Charlotte far more strongly than it presents Jerry: once the cruise scenes are over and Charlotte has returned to Boston, the empowerment gained from her relationship with Jerry is manifested not by his presence but in his absence. Charlotte's independence, from her mother and ultimately from the prospect of security provided by Elliot Livingston, is generated from the self-esteem Jerry has given her, and not merely from how she feels about him, particularly as he is not there for her to rely on.

Both Maria LaPlace and Jeanne Allen, in her introduction to the screenplay, present independence as a strong element in the reading of *Now, Voyager*. Allen suggests that the film offers "something rare and vital in American mass culture: the story of a woman's struggle to gain initiation into adulthood and a relative measure of independence."[11] LaPlace describes the film as being centred around the "representation of female sexuality and questions of female independence and autonomy," ideas which are linked together by the issue fundamental to women's film, that of female desire.[12] She finds Charlotte's repression symptomatic of her lack of independence from her mother and from her family in the broader sense. Indeed, Olive Higgins Prouty describes Charlotte's story as being of "an escape from domestic tyranny."[13] If the film chronicles Charlotte's journey to be cured, a reasonable premise given that Dr. Jaquith's diagnosis of her breakdown opens the film's narrative, then part of her healing will be achieved through her "reliance on her own will and judgement."[14] Charlotte's assertion of her will, firstly against her mother, then against Dr. Jaquith with regard to Tina, and finally against Jerry in resisting their relationship so that she may have the family life she desires with Tina, marks stages in her voyage to confirm her autonomy.[15]

The symbolism of the family is continuous in the film: Charlotte's breakdown signals the friction between her and the head of the family, Mrs. Vale; she is rescued by a 'fairy godmother' in the form of her sister-in-law Lisa, although she is victimised by the wicked niece, Lisa's daughter June. Most significant in this early part of the film is the good father figure—LaPlace describes him as a paternal substitute—Dr. Jaquith, a rare man in the early scenes dominated by authoritative and strident women. After her return from the cruise Charlotte faces her startled family, including rather old-fashioned brothers and their wives, winning them over with her new found confidence. Once Mrs. Vale dies, shocked by Charlotte's rejection of Elliot Livingston's ready-made family, Charlotte finds herself in a position to become a mother herself, as she forms a relationship with Jerry's daughter, Tina. The last scenes of the film, when Charlotte tells Jerry that her house is his home, for "there are people here who love you,"[16] present an alternative to the film's opening: "the miserable matriarchy of the film's beginning has been substituted by a real one. The space has been transformed into one of laughter, light, music and gaiety."[17]

Furthermore, Charlotte is clinging to her independence by refusing to have a relationship with Jerry, or to "find some man who'll make you happy," as Jerry pleads her to do at the film's end.[18] Jeanine Basinger suggests that normally women in film had to sacrifice their own lives and desires to those of the society around them, or more specifically of the men in their lives: "this is part of the rules of behavior that women have to learn in order to survive, or at least to get along in the world."[19] She also suggests, however, that there is an exception to this situation, when a woman's nobility of purpose leads her to sacrifice marriage and conventional female behaviour for the 'greater good' of serving "causes that are deemed suitable for the feminine presence."[20] In *Now, Voyager* Charlotte does not stop loving Jerry, but she rejects him in order that she might serve the higher purpose of assuring Tina's happiness. She sacrifices marriage for motherhood, although neither of these states would have been conventional in themselves. The search for a satisfactory solution to the story is characterised by the juxtaposition of male and female ideals of what constitutes acceptable social and domestic goals: Caryl Flinn suggests that *Now, Voyager*, like other contemporary films such as *Penny Serenade* (1941), exists as "a set of competing, contradictory utopias that work together to defer any sense of final resolution."[21]

The positive twist on Charlotte's feminism of choice can be reversed by considering the roles of the male characters in the film. *Now, Voyager*, with its plot twist of adultery, inspired the publicists to construct imagery which emphasised Davis as the manipulative vamp-bitch figure. Most of the film's advertising posters show Davis in a glamorous black gown, looking sensual and provocative, flanked by lines such as: "She didn't know where she was drifting—

and she didn't care!"; "Every woman has a right to one mistake . . . and I'm not sorry for mine!"; "Don't pity me . . . in our few moments together I found the joy that most women can only dream of!"[22]   It is possible to read Charlotte's transgressive seduction of Jerry, intentional or otherwise depending on how influenced one is by the film's publicity, as ultimately paid for by her taking on the responsibility of adoptive motherhood.   In an article on the common structures of Hollywood melodramas, Barbara Creed finds this atonement or punishment for 'sins' to be a feature of several of Davis's films, particularly *The Old Maid, Dark Victory* and *Now, Voyager*: "[w]omen, by virtue of their role which is related to sexuality, love, marriage and motherhood, are only of dramatic interest when they are at odds with that role, are punished . . . and finally capitulate."[23]   This does not, however, reflect the intentions of Davis's characters to assume and redefine their female roles.   In the context of Charlotte's thwarted encounter with Leslie Trotter on her first cruise, the opportunity to redefine and control her relationships with men later in the film takes   on   greater   significance.   Charlotte's   actions,   however   socially transgressive, have positive consequences: once she is "cured" she begins to act in her own interests, not selfishly, but with self-confidence.   Even Dr. Jaquith is affected by this, for although he shows Charlotte the way to regain and redevelop her   identity,   he   ultimately   becomes   embraced   by   her   new   self-confident objectives, relating to Tina and finally to his sanitarium, Cascade, itself.

Charlotte's redefinition of female roles—inspiring Jerry to return to his beloved architecture, adopting his child, Tina, influencing Jaquith's therapeutic strategies—can   be   read   as   part   of   an   overall   narrative   scheme   of parent/child/spouse   relationships.[24]   Jeanne   Allen   describes   Charlotte   as "nurturing   mother   and . . . peer,"   roles   which   emphasise   Charlotte's   'success' when compared with the 'failures' of her own mother and Tina's mother; however,   both   Jaquith   and   Jerry   assume   parent/spouse   relationships   with Charlotte, which arguably are essential to making her evolution possible at all. Charlotte's journey to empowerment can be viewed entirely in the context of her fulfilling the expectations of both men: Richard Dyer suggests that the narrative "details Davis's liberation from the dowdy spinster role imposed upon her, yet it is a man, a psychiatrist (Claude Rains), who 'gives' her the 'means' to be free, and a man (Paul Henreid) who provides her with her ultimate project in life, namely, his daughter."[25]

Yet it is Charlotte's decision to question the expectations of Elliot Livingston, which seems to mark a moment when she decides to take responsibility for her independence. It would have been an interesting plot resolution were the film to have ended with Charlotte compromising with her mother on the 'acceptable' matrimony to Livingston and compromising her wilful independence by settling down into his family. The relationship with Jerry Durrance would have become merely a stepping stone to Charlotte's self-confidence, a rite of passage between repressed spinsterhood and fulfilled marriage and parenthood. Yet the tones in which her voice-over tells Dr. Jaquith of the relationship indicate the lack of passion in their relationship, and instead the relationship with Elliot Livingston becomes the stepping stone to Charlotte's real independence from her mother.[26] The decision to break her engagement to Elliot ends the truce with her mother in a dramatic and irretrievable manner.

Where Elliot slips out of the front door with a handshake to the strains of Tchaikovsky, Mrs. Vale slips down her chair and out of this life to the sound of Charlotte's fury that her life "has been a calamity on both sides."[27] So the unconsummated romance with Elliot inadvertently forces Charlotte to reckon up her life, without the opposition of her mother to reckon against, and without Jerry, who has allowed her "to marry that man and have a full and happy life."[28]

Now, Voyager set a precedent for later films in its integration of a psychiatric perspective into the narrative. Only a few years later, films such as *Spellbound* (1945) and *Possessed* (1948) were exploring the psychological experiences of women, yet *Now, Voyager* takes only tentative steps in this direction, for Dr. Jaquith's influence is ultimately absorbed by Charlotte's greater self-confidence. In his article on the role of therapy in the film, R. Barton Palmer suggests that the importance of the psychiatric element is preserved from the original novel, rather than being a function of the influence of the "male therapeutic gaze."[29] Furthermore, he argues that the psychiatric component of the film is a male attempt to solve a female question of social, emotional and sexual desire, which is doomed to failure as soon as it succeeds:

the recuperation suggested by her psychiatrist leads Charlotte Vale to abandon the asexuality of premature sisterhood and become a woman who desires and is desired; but Charlotte's desire, once expressed, is immediately identified by the narrative as transgression. The story then leads back to a spinsterhood whose emptiness and social anomaly are denied by the metaphor of "platonic marriage" which seeks but fails to contain it.[30]

Palmer sees a certain equality in the way the film resolves Charlotte's dilemma: she has become a "functioning and useful adult," which he interprets as a neo-Freudian goal, but she has employed her mothering skills to create a supportive home environment out of the formerly cold Vale mansion, within which Tina can be healed by remaining with Charlotte, rather than being sent out on a journey from Jaquith's (male) sanitarium, as Charlotte was herself.[31] The camping trip is a point of departure for this equality, as Charlotte takes Tina away on a trip from Cascade, so they can play at being a family.

Palmer makes explicit the connection between Charlotte's mental health and her sexual attractiveness, but her clothing can be incorporated into this relationship: at the opening of the film, she is frumpy and mentally unstable; her appearance in the ship's cocktail bar in glamorous but borrowed clothes occurs at a time when she is healing but "not well yet";[32] when she returns to Boston her mother tries to force her back into the black and white foulard dress, just as her insensitivity to her daughter's illness undermines Charlotte's confidence; the same evening Charlotte finds resolve and looks stunning in her new black gown; after her mother dies she goes to Cascade ostensibly to have another breakdown, but looks so smart in her suit and hat that Miss Trask barely recognises her, and soon she is distracted from her anxiety by Tina. The importance of self-image is stressed by Davis herself in an interview for the Pressbook:

I have to be overweight and dowdy, and later on I wear beautiful clothes and I'm dressed up, according to Ilka Chase standards. But the real change is a psychological one. This isn't just a story of a worm emerging from a chrysalis and becoming a butterfly. That's what makes it interesting.[33]

Maria LaPlace emphasises the importance of the Pressbook interviews and articles in completing the circular connection between the psychiatric element, the successful progression of the narrative, and the marketability of the film to women: she argues that "Charlotte's cure, then, is first and foremost a transformation of her appearance. . . . [which allows] the next phase of her cure, the love of a good man."[34] Charlotte's rite of passage itself becomes circular, as she completes the film in psychological control of her life, a good parent to Tina, but physically more homely and less glamorous than at any other time since her transformation. She no longer needs to be stunningly dressed, for Jerry must decide whether he will accept Charlotte's terms, on her territory. It is now Tina who is clothed attractively in her "first party dress," and Charlotte steps back from the limelight as her negotiations with social acceptability become less relevant. Just as Tina asks her father, "Do you really like me?", Charlotte no longer needs to, for she can be herself.[35]

Readings of Davis's Performance

Many critics have suggested the importance of Bette Davis herself in the characterisation of a woman seeking her independence. Maria LaPlace describes a "Bette Davis discourse," which emphasises women's struggles for economic and social power. Davis's battles with Warner Brothers over her contractual situation, and her rebellion at the mediocrity of some of the roles she was forced to play, brought her great notoriety in the business for seeking a greater recognition and recompense for Hollywood's leading ladies.[36] Jeanne Allen shows how Davis's personal life reflected the role-breaking independence Charlotte Vale achieves in the film:

Davis's mother became the 'wife' of the professional actress, while Davis felt she had to be father to her mother and sister after her own father left the family. At the same time she tried to be wife to a series of husbands who had to cope with the role of "Mr Davis."[37]

Richard Dyer, adopting Molly Haskell's definition, defines Davis's roles as superfemale:

a woman who, while exceedingly feminine and flirtatious, is too ambitious and intelligent for the docile role society has decreed she play. . . . She remains within traditional society, but having no worthwhile project for her creative energies, turns them onto the only available material—the people around her—with demonic results.[38]

He cites Davis's portrayals of Julie Marston in *Jezebel* (1938), Judith Traherne in *Dark Victory* (1939), and Mildred in *Of Human Bondage* (1934), among others, as examples of such a woman; clearly Charlotte Vale does not fit with this identity, suggesting that *Now, Voyager* is not typical of Davis's work. Certainly, Charlotte is no 'bitch,' nor is she a manipulative *femme fatale* giving female strength a bad name. This certainly goes against the publicity for the film: in one poster Davis is reclining, cigarette in hand, careless expression on face, beside the caption "don't blame me for what happened . . . It happens in the best of families!" Davis's pose is not one taken from the film, and arguably the marketing of the two stars doesn't match the film much either: "Bette Davis, more radiant, more exciting than ever—in love with Paul Henreid, the man, at last, to match her every emotion."[39] Yet, as with many other Warner films of the time, Charlotte must submit to the will of society, creating acceptable narrative closure at the end of the film by conforming to a more acceptable role.[40] Where in *Jezebel*, *Dark Victory* and *Of Human Bondage*, not to mention the dramatic *In This Our Life* (1941), Davis's transgressor dies, in *Now, Voyager* she accepts her lot, gives up her man and accepts the definition of motherhood.

Much of the evolution of Charlotte's character in the film can be shown through the use of dialogue, and the extent of her involvement in it. The first scenes of the film, until Charlotte's appearance on the boat, have very little of Charlotte speaking, except in the flashback sequence, and her state of mind is communicated principally through her emphatic silences and a few careful sentences. This restraint is maintained until the scene on the ship's deck when Charlotte shows Jerry her family picture, and she begins to speak more freely as she unburdens herself. The degrees of articulacy and limitation jostle with one another, alternating between the scenes with Jerry and those with her mother and Elliot Livingston, until finally at Cascade with Tina she seems more fluent. As she begins to assume a mothering role, her dialogue, and the delivery with which Davis empowers it, becomes more assured and smooth, as Charlotte is no longer using her words to articulate the uncertainties in her personality. Her verbal relationship with Tina is based on certainties, particularly her questioning of Tina in the cafe and her comforting of the child after the nightmare. This leads into a dialogue of equals with Dr. Jaquith, and finally the same with Jerry.

Olive Higgins Prouty suggested that the most successful cinematic version of *Now, Voyager* might be made as a silent film: "the acting, facial expressions, every move and gesture is more significant and far more closely observed by an audience waiting for the explanatory caption or voice," although clearly this was not adopted.[41] In this respect, the choice of Bette Davis is highly appropriate for the lead role: her acting style used a very wide range of facial expressions to dominate silences, and this physical presence was complemented by a broad compass of enunciation to bring dramatic emphasis to dialogue. Her clipped New England accent balanced an almost musical undulation in tone to make her more intense speeches almost operatic. The scene at the railway station, where Charlotte tries to convince Jerry that he has made a difference to her life, is a fine example of how the dialogue represents the development in the character's social discourse. The sequence of scenes leading up to this begins in her mother's room where she is arranging roses and enjoying a slightly terse exchange of views about Elliot's proposal of marriage. Charlotte's reserve is stretched in the cab where she tries to explain to Elliot her concerns about moving into his family life, but she retains her quiet poise of equanimity, while the voice over reminds us that her thoughts are still with a lover whose name cannot be spoken. This duality of dialogue is resumed in the next scene at the cocktail party where Charlotte meets Jerry again. Their double exchange of dry, innocuous small talk and impassioned whispers, as text and subtext, throws the formality of Charlotte's relationship with Elliot into relief against the liberating influence of Jerry. The way in which this sequence ends, with Charlotte's fervent protestations to a rather wooden Jerry of the way his love has given her the strength to go on with her life, completes the sphere of emotion experienced by

Charlotte's evolution in just a short time. Even when, in the next scene, Charlotte tries to explain her need for passion to Elliot, she is unable to evoke more than a shadow of her earlier vehemence with Jerry, and the emotion instead comes pouring out in her argument with Mrs. Vale.

Readings of Characterisation

Now, Voyager is a film with a comparatively small cast of principals, with the action revolving around Charlotte's relationships with four other characters. The marketing of the film implies that it should be seen as a love story, a chronicle of the relationship between Charlotte and Jerry, but he does not appear until almost 25 minutes into the film, and only reappears at the end after being almost entirely absent for all the action between Charlotte and Tina. It seems more accurate to suggest that the relationship can be read as indicative of Charlotte's evolution, a journey initiated by her mother, facilitated by Dr. Jaquith, sustained by Jerry and reaching fruition through Tina. Mrs. Vale opens the film, imposing her personality on the servants and then on Lisa and Dr. Jaquith. Her manner is unquestionably direct and authoritative, and she treats Charlotte with a lack of sympathy and understanding. In fact, Mrs. Vale is hostile to the entire scenario, from Lisa's well meaning intervention to Jaquith's representation of the medical profession. She is queen and mistress of her domain, strolling regally in her long gowns and sitting with poise in the straight-backed chair. Her attempts to reassert authority over Charlotte on her return from the cruise form some of the most dramatic scenes of the film. After the romance, passion and flowering of Charlotte's personality, all accompanied by lush music from Steiner, the scene with her mother is tense and confrontational, with stark black and white costumes and no music. This is, after all, the first juxtaposition of the root of Charlotte's anxiety with her own attempts at resolving it. Charlotte has become a different person, most strikingly in image, yet her mother wastes no time in delineating the old mould into which the new Charlotte must fit. The battle is played out in several stages, and in each of them Mrs. Vale asserts a different element of her controlling wisdom: Charlotte's clothes, her bedroom, her financial security, her relationship, and finally the purpose of her life. She deludes us into thinking that she may have compromised slightly with Charlotte over Elliot Livingston, in the roses scene noted above, but ultimately this concession becomes the foundation of their most profound and fatal disagreement.

Mrs. Vale becomes a symbol against which Charlotte's evolution is measured, and the extent of their disagreements and compromises are a barometer for Charlotte's independence. Charlotte is perhaps finally measured against Mrs. Vale because she elects the role of motherhood. Her identification, early on in her relationship with Jerry, that Tina was not wanted by her mother establishes an irresistible connection between Charlotte and the child, one which is crying out to be resolved for both their benefits. Charlotte's ability to make up for the shortcomings of her own mother in her parenting of Tina provides a context for this resolution, although Charlotte is careful to portray herself as 'aunt' rather than substitute mother as far as Tina is concerned. There is a distorted symmetry here with the early scenes between Charlotte and her real niece, June: at the beginning of the film, Charlotte's view of herself as a spinster aunt is defined by the enmity between her and June, and the younger woman's spiteful humour about Charlotte's single status. Later on, this single status is what makes the 'aunt' relationship between Charlotte and Tina possible, one which is defined by their unconditional love for each other.

Dr. Jaquith also provides a standard against which Charlotte can measure herself, although the nature of their relationship changes during the film. His easy conversational gambits at the beginning of the film become an equal dialogue by the time Charlotte challenges him regarding Tina, and in the end, even though Jaquith's moral position dictates Charlotte's relationship with Jerry, it is she who seems to be in control of their discussion about Cascade. It is Jaquith's kindness to her in the beginning which emphasises the inadequacy of Mrs. Vale's behaviour, and he becomes a 'good father' figure almost by default. His careful compliments of her ivory carving, and his deliberate demarcation of her life as private, mark out the standards by which he expects Mrs. Vale to behave, standards to which he alludes without embarrassment in their showdown. Charlotte's timidity and deference towards Jaquith in the scenes prior to the cruise further support this parent/child metaphor, a hierarchy that is maintained through Jaquith's voice-overs and Charlotte's letter to him. It is difficult therefore to isolate the moment at which she begins to assert herself in the relationship: the scene at Cascade when she criticises him for the way Tina has been handled shows that things are different between them, but the nature of Charlotte's growing up in relation to her 'father' is undefined.[42] Jaquith certainly facilitates Charlotte's voyage to independence, but he also places boundaries on it by making explicit the trade-off between Jerry and Tina. So, as Richard Dyer points out, a man gives her the means to be free, but he also provides the choice between the 'restrictions' of love or motherhood.

Charlotte's relationship with Jerry Durrance is defined by the give and take between them. Jerry gives Charlotte an opportunity to confess to who she is, he gives her admiration, respect and love; she gives him a chance to express himself romantically and humorously, and also gives him back the interest he had in architecture; he gives her Tina, by sending the child to Dr. Jaquith; she gives him a home to be a family with his child in. Indeed, Caryl Flinn suggests that Jerry's willingness to take part in family life and his concern as a parent "establish him as [a] 'utopian' 'sensitive male'."[43] It is quite easy to see Jerry as simply the lover, giving Charlotte a reason to go on living, but what Charlotte does for Jerry not only improves the quality of his life, but of hers as well. Jerry underestimates Charlotte when he evaluates her needs as being to find "some man who will make you happy," for as Charlotte tells Dr. Jaquith, she needs to be needed too.[44] As far as Jaquith is concerned, this refers to her parenting of Tina, but her relationship with Jerry is one of equality, and Charlotte actively recognises what is important to Jerry. In the scene at the railway station, Jerry tells her how their relationship has made him kinder to his wife, and one can equate this with Charlotte's remarks about finding the strength to go into the lion's den: their love has given them both something to build on in their old lives.

It is this equality which emphasises the difference between Charlotte's relationships with Jerry and with Elliot. Elliot has a ready-made family, he will build her a new house, he has much to offer, but he does not seem to need anything in return. One can only assume that his search for a new wife is being made for social reasons, rather than being a more fundamental drive for companionship.   The ease with which he suggests altering the cruise arrangements from two tickets to three, as they break off their engagement, suggests that this is merely an inconvenience, rather than a major emotional tear. Although Charlotte talks rather obliquely of her desires in their awkward post-concert conversation, Elliot is simply not in tune with Charlotte's needs or, more fundamentally, with who she is. This has made a startling contrast with the scene between Jerry and Charlotte on the cruise ship when she shows him her photograph album and the truth about her breakdown comes out. Jerry takes the revelations very comfortably: he is not appalled or startled, and his letter to Tina that night reflects his complete understanding of Charlotte's situation.

Tina is, conversely, rather unnerved by Charlotte's immediate sympathy and understanding when they first meet at Cascade, to the extent that she tries to disarm Charlotte by guessing at who she is. The screenplay notes, "A most piteously unattractive child, the sight of whom has startled Charlotte."[45] Then, describing Charlotte's actions, "Tina looks up then, quickly and suspiciously. How well Charlotte recognizes the feelings from her own childhood that have made her look up this way."[46] Their conversation is aggressive on Tina's part, hesitant but rather practical on Charlotte's; almost immediately Charlotte sets about trying to make Tina's life more bearable. The intervention with Miss Trask over the table tennis game and the conspicuous half truth about taking the car to the garage make Charlotte's motives extremely clear, and yet she is uncertain about exactly how to behave with Tina. What makes this relationship interesting is that both characters are learning about themselves and each other, in contrast to Charlotte's relationships with the other principals, each of whom was quite confident in himself or herself. Charlotte has no idea how to show Tina that she cares, and the scene in the cafe shows her feeling her way around trying to get Tina to express her anxieties. When Tina really opens up, in the night-time scene, Charlotte finds herself drawn into intimate proximity to the child, a far cry from the rather formal exchange that took place in the cafe. In trying to explain to Tina why she is being kind to her, Charlotte refers to the kindness of someone else (Jerry) who helped her; this mirrors Jerry's letter to Tina from the cruise ship where he obliquely refers to Charlotte's situation in trying to explain to Tina why she felt lonely.

Tina becomes rapidly secure in Charlotte's company, from the tennis game to the camping trip, and Charlotte becomes more confident in evaluating what is best for the girl. However, this confidence is only gained in the context of Dr. Jaquith's permission, firstly to take Tina camping, and secondly to take her back to the Vale mansion in Boston. In this latter scene, at a campsite, Tina and Charlotte seem comfortable together, but they have different ways of acknowledging the success of their relationship. After reminding Tina that they have no secrets from one another, Charlotte tells Tina that she wants to take her home to Boston: "it would be sort of like playing house."[47] Tina translates this into parental terms, but Charlotte is quick to present herself as no contest to her real mother, but simply as a sort of friend. The way in which she provides Tina with clothes and a studio seems more in the nature of an interested philanthropist than a parent, and the party that is being held in the last section of the film implies that Charlotte is a benevolent hostess for young people. This is, however, a clear separation from what she really feels, as she acknowledges in her final remarks to Jerry about Tina being their child. Perhaps the success of Charlotte's parenting of Tina is that she does not really behave like a parent, but more as an unconditional friend. She opens up her life and her home to provide Tina with all the opportunities that she could want as a child, while maintaining a sense of proportion over the way in which Tina relates to her. Charlotte is therefore living out her desires in a controlled way, but with the satisfaction of knowing that she has made a difference to the lives of herself, Tina and Jerry.

—————— Chapter 4 ——————

THE MUSIC AND ITS CONTEXT

Once again Max Steiner assists mood and dramatic intent by giving this picture a symphonic musical background of impressive strength. The love poem filtering through the superb action is a symphonic tone poem of great beauty, stressing a great spiritual quality. The ratio between dialogue and music and action is well defined at all times, yet music is an important dramatic element, eloquently supporting description, emotion, action, mood and pace. The work is heavily orchestrated in keeping with the weight of the story, varying in range to contrast with the production structure.

—Newspaper Review of *Now, Voyager* [1]

THE MUSIC

From the opening of the film, with its bold orchestral statement, to the quotation of popular hits of the day, the score for *Now, Voyager* relishes the power of music to be expressive. Steiner has seized the opportunity to create a score which, though largely non-diegetic, emphasises our experience of the characters from points of view both within and outside the narrative space. Where the diegetic choices for the cruise ship cocktail bar, the party, the cafe near Cascade and the Vale mansion evoke quite particular atmospheres and contexts for the action, the non-diegetic score seems to traverse and transcend the narrative boundaries that can make a post-production score seem objective and wise after the event.

It is easy to underestimate the problems facing the composer in creating a structure for a score that responds to the film but does not overplay the composer's advantage in knowing the film in its entirety. A score which employs the thematic approach that Steiner relies on needs to take account of the pace of revelation of plot developments, and the ways in which characters evolve and become challenged by events during the course of the film. The narrative of *Now, Voyager* encompasses a long period of narrative development and a range of different geographical localities, as well as the interplay between a number of characters. Steiner's score is successful in managing the responses to these diverse elements within one main approach to scoring, the employment of memorable melodic ideas.

Arguably, this film is dominated by its music, and it might easily be *Now, Voyager* that Hans Keller had in mind when he berated Hollywood composers for overscoring.[2] The complex patchwork of thematic quotation, which is the backdrop for much of the action, might be unheard by the average audience member, making Steiner's precision construction completely irrelevant. By contrast, the placement of music is clearly effective. The use of pauses in the middle of long sections of music and the lengthy segments of unscored film create a sense of expectation and fulfillment about the music when it is used. For example, most of the conversations between Charlotte and Mrs. Vale are unaccompanied by music, but in the scene when Mrs. Vale is explaining her will, her theme is used, orchestrated for brass. This statement of instrumental grandeur evokes the power of Mrs. Vale and implies the prospect of Charlotte being wealthy and influential. Yet in their final scene together, where they are arguing about Charlotte breaking her engagement to Elliot, the battle for control over Charlotte's life remains uninterpreted by music until after Mrs. Vale has died. Steiner also uses silence, particularly in the form of the pause, as musical punctuation, for example when Charlotte has finished explaining about her breakdown to Jerry. Like a moment of calm after the storm, the pause reflects Charlotte regaining her composure; it also highlights the introduction of the "love" theme as new to the score, and marks a new level of intimacy between Charlotte and Jerry.

Steiner's approach has been described as "hyperexplicit," using music to indicate as much as it is able to in as literal terms as possible.[3] This can take different forms, such as mickey-mousing (the mimicry of movement) or intellectual signposting (the use of music as connotative or symbolic): the two metallic chimes of celeste and xylophone mickey-mouse the coins dropping into the phone box when Tina first calls her father from the cafe; alternatively, the short quotation from "Yankee Doodle Dandy" marks the return of the cruise ship to New York, signalled visually by the shot of the Statue of Liberty. Steiner's methodical interpretation of action through placement of musical themes can also be read as hyper-explicit, leading us on a journey through the story as explained by the different themes. Such an approach arguably leaves little room for music to be an ambiguous narrative agent, and when the themes relate to particular characters, we have an almost complete version of the story in music. Analysis of the score for *Now, Voyager* shows this to be the case, particularly because Steiner has coupled definition of all the major characters with expression of their emotional experiences.

Steiner's greatest achievement in this score is the variety of ways in which he balances the scheme of thematic meaning with the sound of the music. Irrespective of our ability as an audience to respond to the minutiae, we are swept along by the feel of the score. Listening to it as music alone, one can experience quite directly moments of heightening tension and of the onset of hysteria, but when coupled with the visuals and overlaid with dialogue, the music still has an impact. Much of this effect can be attributed to the use of pitch

contours in the score: the rising or falling of both thematic lines and more fragmented textures emphasises the emotional contours of the characters' experiences. From the small-scale falling contour of Charlotte's theme to the strong ascension of Dr. Jaquith's theme, Steiner manipulates the contours to express the relative characterisations and to redefine and apply the thematic ideas as the narrative develops. The underlying language of harmonic ambiguity or diatonic stability also gives a feeling for the emotional complexity of the characters. The most 'singable' of the themes are Mrs. Vale's and the love theme, with their simple scalic designs. By contrast, the comparative harmonic and chromatic complexities of Charlotte's and Dr. Jaquith's themes reflect these characters' more complicated personalities and situations. This implies a hierarchy of emotional norms reflected in musical norms, where emotional stability is equated with the diatonic, and psychological tension with chromaticism and harmonic ambiguity.

The score also uses rhythm and tempo to great effect: when we first see Charlotte walking down the stairs, the cross rhythms of the theme seem not only to drag with her feet, but to slow her down with uncertainty as she approaches her mother; by contrast, when she leaves the room soon afterwards in a state of hysteria and agitation, the the music is characterised by a frantic pace and short rhythmic motifs. Charlotte's joy at Jerry's gift of perfume, and the measured enthusiasm of her consequent preparations for dinner are matched by a melodic idea which starts steadily and gathers pace through use of triplets and dotted rhythms; the good humour and enjoyment of both the tennis game and the camping trip are also evoked by fast-moving rhythms. This superficial mood of the score contrasts with the specific musical designs and underpins Steiner's success as a film composer. He writes music that can bear considerable detailed analysis but which does not require it in order to be understood in its immediate filmic context.

This combination of the apparent and the obscure, the fusing of simplicity and explicit expression with complex development and manipulation, seem at once to woo and alienate the listener. Steiner has been as unsubtle in his rendering of Tina's footsteps as she runs down the stairs to greet her father as he has been ingenious in the delay to the cadence that underscores Charlotte's discussion of Elliot's proposal with her mother, and they represent extremes of his approach. The tinkling footsteps seem almost facile and obvious to the more sophisticated late twentieth century audience; by contrast, the evasive cadential chord is almost inaudible, yet narratively they have the same effect, expressing the characters as they would express themselves. Tina lacks sophistication and ambiguity: her tears and interrogation of those around her show the innocence of the child she is. The chiming money in the telephone and Tina's footsteps are as transparent as she is. Conversely, Charlotte's relationship with Elliot is based on his ability to accept her for who she is, creating a relationship which requires negotiation: the total absence of original non-diegetic music for Charlotte and Elliot, and the use instead of the 'borrowed' Tchaikovsky, the first movement of the "Pathétique" Sixth Symphony, reveals their relationship as a shadow of the passion found between Charlotte and Jerry. The displacement of the Tchaikovsky into objectified experiences—the concert and the radio—denies the immediacy of non-diegetic commentary: we can feel the emotion of the love

between Charlotte and Jerry because the non-diegetic score specifically invites us to experience it first hand; we can only hear the Tchaikovsky through shared diegetic ears, and it becomes distanced from us. However, this interaction between music and action is constructed with complexity, and though the sterility of Charlotte and Elliot's music is apparent, its parodic relationship with the love theme is less so.

NOW, VOYAGER'S MUSICAL ANTECEDENTS

Steiner was extremely busy in 1941 and 1942, acting as principal composer for at least twelve films during that period. Letters he sent to his third wife, Louise Klos Steiner, vividly reflect the daily grind of studio work and the lack of artistic control.[4]

Well darling, I have to go into the projection room and look at "Now, Voyager", the new Betty Davis [sic] picture, and so will close. [16 June 1942]

They previewed my picture again last night and the audience stood up at the end and cheered. Warner said that it is the greatest music score that has ever been in any picture—marvelous. I didn't think much of it when I saw it which should prove that I should stick to my fiddle and try not to be a producer. [18 June 1942][5]

I am trying to finish "Watch on the Rhine" by Saturday, and I have three reels to go; probably the most difficult job I have ever had. It is just like the "Informer", the only difference being that I have even less time on this one and I am dead tired from the other pictures. [7 October 1942]

I am working on "Mark Twain" and it is a tremendous job, but I have five reels recorded, and everybody thinks it is a pretty good job. I still have ten reels to go, and I am so tired from writing so much music. It is an awful hard road and I am so bored with the piano that I cannot look at it. [24 November 1942]

There are no interviews with Steiner published contemporary to the release of *Now, Voyager,* nor is the score for the film discussed in *Notes to You*; however it is clear from the vast majority of the scores he wrote in the early 1940s that the thematic approach found in *Now, Voyager* was a technique he felt comfortable using for a variety of film genres. The music for *Dr. Ehrlich's Magic Bullet* and *The Letter* (both 1940), *The Great Lie* (1941), *They Died with Their Boots On, The Gay Sisters* and *In This Our Life* (all 1942) all bear comparison with *Now, Voyager*: expansive soundscapes using themes to express characterisation. The scores for *In This Our Life* and *They Died with Their Boots On* share the clearest similarities with *Now, Voyager*: each score uses a thematic scheme to capture the strong central characters, and the themes are designed with explicit references to diatonic and chromatic contrasts. *In This Our Life* and *They Died with Their Boots On* both feature good and bad characters in opposition to each other, and Steiner has relished the opportunitity to paint these extremes musically.[6] Steiner has created more variation in his use of Custer's theme (*They Died with Their Boots On*) than of Stanley Timberlake's (*In This Our Life*) or Charlotte Vale's. The simplicity of the Custer motif, an ascending

leap of a perfect fifth, allows for greater development and variation, and Steiner is able to match the changes in the character's fortune by contracting and expanding the perfect fifth and by changing the harmony from major to minor. By contrast, the themes for Bette Davis's characters are complex, for the motives and experiences of Stanley and Charlotte are not as transparent as Custer's. While the motifs are inherently intricate, their developments are correspondingly limited, and Steiner solves the narrative dilemmas these designs propose quite differently: Stanley never changes or shows remorse for what she has done, so Steiner is not obliged to develop her theme; Charlotte however does change, but rather than develop her theme, Steiner uses it less and eventually uses other themes to represent facets of her experience.

Similarly, Steiner employs the diatonic-chromatic scheme to capture the range of behaviour exhibited by the three protagonists of these films: Custer is a bold, if occasionally misguided hero, and his theme is only rarely tainted by chromatic association; Stanley is a self-centred villain, and her theme clearly enjoys the extremes of expression that the chromatic intervals provide; Charlotte is neither hero nor villain, treading a narrow path between unfortunate victim and deliberate adultress, and it is the tension between diatonic and chromatic which captures the ambiguity that Charlotte experiences. The similarities with *Now, Voyager* lie not in the detail but in the spirit with which the thematic approach is adopted. In each of these scores, as in many others, Steiner seems to relish the challenge of seeking out expressions of the characters and harnessing musical language to create them.

The richness of orchestration found in *Now, Voyager* has a precedent in *The Letter*. The latter score is one of Steiner's most powerful, although the film presents a contrasting challenge to *Now, Voyager*. Davis plays a woman trapped by the consequences of her actions—adultery, deceit, murder: the comparative thematic simplicity of the score captures the claustrophobia of Davis's character and the lack of progress her character makes during the story; its only outlet is found in the intensity of the orchestral texture. The diversity of instrumentation used in *Now, Voyager* is also similar to that employed for *Casablanca*. Both films juxtapose the demands of 'foreign' musical cultures of South America and North Africa with the familiarity of popular jazz ensembles and conventional non-diegetic film orchestras.

In terms of the volume of music required, the short scores for *They Died with Their Boots On, The Gay Sisters, Desperate Journey, Now, Voyager* and *The Adventures of Mark Twain* are all over one hundred and seventy pages in length, constituting substantial investments of time and effort.[7] Each of these films suffers a degree of narrative fragmentation, and the music becomes a coherent force to bridge broad passages of time—such as in the biographical pictures *They Died with Their Boots On* and *The Adventures of Mark Twain*—or to bring together the common aims of diverse characters—as in *The Gay Sisters* and *Desperate Journey*. However, the list of films Steiner scored in 1941 and 1942 shows how broadly he cast his style: for *The Adventures of Mark Twain* he wrote music to evoke striking atmospheric effects and to mickey-mouse the humour of the story; humour also characterises the score for *The Gay Sisters*, although, like that of *Casablanca*, this score is virtually monothematic in the simplicity of its melodic structure. *Desperate Journey* and *Captains of the Clouds* are both wartime Air Force action films, and in writing the scores for both films Steiner had to contend with a considerable soundtrack of aircraft and automobile engine noises. The score for *Desperate Journey* particularly relishes the symbolism and association of national and partisan anthems; these clearly recognisable tunes are contrasted with the central theme of this film, which is defined rhythmically and atmospherically rather than melodically, capturing the tension which propels the action almost from the outset. The non-diegetic music for *In This Our Life* parodies the diegetic contemporary dance music, while *Watch on the Rhine* has a sparse soundtrack, sensitive to the theatrical pacing of the film, derived from its origins as a stage play.

STEINER'S INTENTIONS

Apart from a few newspaper articles, there is little published contemporary evidence of how Steiner perceived the role of film music in the years preceding the composition of the score for *Now, Voyager*. In 1935 the *New York Times* published an article entitled "Music in the Cinema: Hollywood Has Discovered How the Score Improves the Photoplay," for which Steiner was interviewed while he completed his score for the RKO film *The Three Musketeers*. The article describes the practice of writing and recording a film score, reporting Steiner's direct involvement with post-composition activities such as conducting, seating of musicians in the dubbing room and evaluating the final balance of the recorded tracks. It also gave him a platform to justify his approach, including the now frequently quoted judgement of the score for *The Informer*: "Every character should have a theme. In 'The Informer' we used a theme to identify Victor McLaglen. A blind man could have sat in a theatre and known when Gypo was on the screen. Music aids audiences in keeping characters straight in their minds."[8] The article also emphasises Steiner's dramatic judgement:

[He] likes pictures with little or no dialogue because he feels that he is contributing more to the drama of the offering. But when characters speak, he often tries to carry the sound of their voices with the instruments, especially in moody scenes where he emphasizes the emotional qualities of the plot himself.[9]

Steiner enjoyed a further flurry of press activity during 1939 and 1940 courtesy of a journalist and academic, Bruno David Ussher, who wrote for a variety of newspapers and magazines including the *Pasadena Star News*, *Los Angeles Daily News* and the *Hollywood Spectator*. Ussher wrote an article about Steiner's music for *Gone with the Wind* in which he establishes the importance of a thematic structure for bringing coherence to the complications of the story: part of the article included an interview with Steiner, and the composer's own comments about the music are as illuminating as the critic's interpretation:

More important than all these individual [characters] is 'Tara', the O'Hara family plantation. Having felt the 'wind', I can grasp that feeling for 'Tara', which moved Scarlett's father and which is one of the finest instincts in her, that love for the soil where she had been born, love of the life before her own which had been founded so strongly. That is why the 'Tara' theme begins and ends the picture and permeates the entire score.[10]

He similarly stresses the importance of the thematic structure in an interview for the *People's Daily World* in September 1939:

In my mind's eye I create themes for the principal characters. I then begin to consider the all-important matter of timing the pace of the film—to speed up gradually towards the climax. . . . Giving the musical score continuity is the great problem of composing film music. There must be never a break that will disturb the easy running of the picture.[11]

In the same article, Steiner indicates that this sacrosanct aim may exist beside a more universal objective, although he seems to express it as a contradiction:

In considering music for films you must divorce the idea of the concert platform from the motion pictures. We are not here to give concerts. The music must be subjugated to the picture. Music builds up moods. . . . I believe that much of the music composed for film backgrounds can stand alone as pure music. . . . Hollywood is composing ever finer music with its films. We are really trying to produce as fine music as possible realizing that the taste for good music will grow the more it is used.[12]

The desire to be taken seriously as a composer of concert hall quality is an element of Steiner's career that bubbles under the surface of his music and is rarely heard beyond that context. Writing film music of value and the need for its subjugation and effective inaudibility created an opposition which drove his work of the late 1930s and early 1940s. The music of that period in particular is crying out to be heard, with its instrumental variety, emphatic placement, dramatic expression and layers of thematic complexity and inter-relation; yet he plays by the rules of orchestration, never allowing the music to clash with a voice or overwhelm a moment, and only rarely to distract the viewer.

This subtext came to the fore on one occasion as a consequence of an article written by Bruno Ussher in the *New York Times* in 1940, entitled "Composing for Films: Opportunities for Creation by Writers of Music in Hollywood," in which he explained the dynamics of the studio-composer relationship which prevented Arnold Schoenberg from engaging in a film scoring project.[13]   Ussher draws a distinction between "personages of the strictly symphonic and operatic realm" and "pioneer film composers," arguing that without the "screen music veterans who have blazed a steep and rocky trail," such as Steiner, Alfred Newman and Hugo Friedhofer, the "second generation of film composers," such as Erich Wolfgang Korngold and Aaron Copland, would not have succeeded in an industry where "the need for and function of music is recognized but rarely understood." Steiner responded to the article in an internal studio memorandum penned with considerable fury:

Some of we "pioneers" are also symphonic composers, having studied at the best musical academies and we are quite capable of writing any kind of symphonic or operatic music if he would want to do so. It is peculiar that none of our ilk who have prepared the ground for symphonic music and who have continually written and are still writing it, are called symphonic composers. A symphonic composer at present is a composer who has never written anything for pictures, and a symphonic composer who is writing for pictures, ceases to be a symphonic composer.[14]

Scores such as *The Letter* or *Now, Voyager* are easily heard as a response to what Steiner seemed to view as latent criticism. The scores for the Bette Davis melodramas in particular employ an almost Tchaikovskian melodic yearning and antiphony between sections of the orchestra. These are expansive works, packed with emotion and structure, hinting at a programme yet demonstrating, as in the case of *Now, Voyager*, a virtually organic interconnection between thematic ideas. This is the music of a composer who wants to be taken seriously by his peers as being capable of drawing on his authentic academic training and bringing well-written music of universal quality to a different context.

Critics and historians of Steiner's music have often come to quite diverse and contradictory conclusions about a connection with the concert hall idiom. Haun and Raborn, writing in *Films in Review* in 1961 suggested that Steiner's music clearly imitates Wagner[15], yet an insensed Tony Thomas responded that Steiner's "turn-of-the-century Viennese quality" made him specifically non-Wagnerian.[16] Both however miss the point that Steiner's capacity to weave the popular songs and styles of the pre-war years into his orchestral scores reveals his experience of musical theatre, not the concert hall. Even with the benefit of hindsight, interviews, articles and *Notes to You*, we cannot be clear about exactly what Steiner intended to achieve with the music for *Now, Voyager*. His remarks about *Gone with the Wind*, particularly the desire for the Tara theme to "permeate" the entire score, might be reviewed in the dominance of Charlotte's theme in *Now, Voyager*: although her motif is replaced later in the film by Tina's theme, its spirit—encapsulated in the falling two-note contour—is felt throughout the score. Steiner's desire to preserve strong characterisation in a thematic response is such a consistent feature of his scores of this period that we can at least judge that his imagination was captured by the people portrayed in this film and that they, as much as the story itself, gave him the raw material for his creativity.

CRITICAL RECEPTION

Contemporary criticism of Steiner in the national newspapers and Hollywood press was generally very good, although film reviews ranged from a paraphrase of the film's credits:

Photography by James Wong Howe is of expected fine standard, as is the music by Max Steiner, arranged by Hugo Friedhofer and directed by Leo F. Forbstein[17]

to more thorough and subjective criticism:

Background music for *We Are Not Alone* demonstrates engagingly that music need not be heavy to be emotionally emphatic. Composer Max Steiner and orchestrator, Hugo Friedhofer, have emulated with artistic fidelity the deftness of touch with which Producer-Director Henry Blanke has bared human tragedy in this picture.[18]

Most reviews however were pitched somewhere between the two:

[the film is as] stirring as the incidental music of Max Steiner.[19]

I might well amend my opinions about Steiner's "Dark Victory" score by saying that upon a second hearing I would possibly consider its emotional dramatic implications as quite sufficient.[20]

If there is such a thing as screenable writing, then there is also photogenic music, a field in which Mr Steiner is a remarkably skilful practitioner. . . . Up to the point in this score where brass bands playing "Hail Columbia," cowboys singing "O Susanna," "Little Brown Jug" and "Dixie" are required by the action, Mr Steiner manages to write five or six minutes of vigorous, richly-scored themes which have valid musical quality as well as relationship to the background of the film.[21]

Exceptional too . . . the haunting emphasis placed upon the drama by the fine musical score of Max Steiner.[22]

Steiner restrained himself in his scoring from dipping into conventional melodic bathos. . . . Perhaps the highest praise which can be given to the Steiner work is that the score never pushes for favor above the dramatic action.[23]

The music by Max Steiner, however, frequently intrudes and by permitting an audience to be conscious of it, underscores dramatic weakness.[24]

The musical background is unobtrusively helpful.[25]

Miss Stanwyck breaks [George] Brent's heart to the accompaniment of "My Mammy Done Tol' Me" on the soundtrack. Whoever thought that up—Max Steiner is listed as responsible for the music—hit upon one of the best laughs of the season, albeit one on the whimsical side.[26]

Bruno Ussher brought an analytical approach to his reviews of Steiner's scores in a series of articles entitled "Cinemusic and Its Meaning," published in various magazines and in pamphlets through the cinema theatre chains, of which the first was on *Gone with the Wind*, as discussed above; a later article was published on the score for *Dr. Ehrlich's Magic Bullet* (1940), which was also given as a lecture. These articles attempt, as their title suggests, to dissect the scores and establish a structure and function for music in the film, blending unabashed praise and adulation with a form of score analysis. Both articles focus specifically on the contribution of the thematic structure of the score:
[Steiner's] capacity for penetrating into the casual ramifications and inner complications of a story and story characters, long proven and proven admirably must have moved Producer David Selznick to bespeak Steiner's services as a composer. That is why Steiner could set as he did the bright, yet pathos-filled, music for this picture. . . . This theme of "Tara" is like a monumental, yet sweetly weaving tree which stands at the very entrance and exit to the house of "Tara." . . . A great music symbol of a theme, grown from the very symbolism of the book and the film "Gone With the Wind."[27]

Steiner has based this long score . . . on a limited number of themes. The effect of the picture is heightened by music of paralleling rather than supplementary meaning. . . . There is [a] healing theme, often heard in the high violoncello position. . . . Clever indeed is the use of bells when Ehrlich, for the first time shows his slide of microbe photographs . . . [which] have a quite evident significance.[28]

The review of *Now, Voyager* quoted at the beginning of this chapter is a tribute to the perfect score and emphasises each of the elements which appear to have been important to Steiner himself. The unobtrusive effectiveness of the music and its steady suitability for the film are marked out for obvious praise, yet it is also measured against external standards of musicianship, in its "symphonic" idiom of orchestration and structure. The score won Steiner an Academy Award, and this newspaper review might easily have been his commendation. There is, however, considerable irony in the adaptation of the love theme from the score into a popular song, with words by Kim Gannon. Entitled "It Can't Be Wrong," the lyrics play on the prospect of forbidden love, creating a connection with the adulterous element of the film's narrative. This made it possible for Steiner to create a satire at his own expense when he used the song as the theme for Mildred's relationship with playboy Monte Beragon in his score for *Mildred Pierce* (1945). While this latter score sustains the principles of *Now, Voyager* in its structure of thematic characterisation and its rich orchestration, the symphonic idiom is subverted by a more popular jazz style, of which "It Can't Be Wrong" seems to be the crowning element. Such brilliant self-mockery would not be possible without the depth of suggestion in the score for *Now, Voyager.*

The music for film has also been the subject of more recent investigation, with strikingly different objectives. Claudia Gorbman used her perception of Steiner as a melodramatic composer, in the principally melodramatic genre of classical Hollywood film, to formulate her exposition of "classical scoring principles."[29] Drawing examples from *King Kong, Of Human Bondage* (1933) and *Mildred Pierce*, she explores Steiner's "voluminous presence and influence" in the scoring practice of the late 1930s and early 1940s, showing how music's key structural and narrative functions are a by-product of Steiner's natural thematic coherence and sense for dramatic emphasis.[30] Although Gorbman is not aiming for a stylistic appraisal of Steiner, her approach does consider how the spectator might experience his music, particularly in the short discussion of the balcony scene in *Now, Voyager.* She describes the range of roles the music plays, from symbolism to continuity, and the inflection of dialogue with "meaning, depth and drama."[31] Most significantly, however, she suggests that the music of this scene is vital in filling the gap between the declaration of love made by Charlotte and Jerry and the emotion and depth their dialogue and physical gestures fail to represent. Although Gorbman does not make the connection, the influence of Lehár and Viennese operetta is apparent in her perception: the richly orchestrated waltz is the love duet of Charlotte and Jerry, their 'song-without-words' that completes their frustrated conversation.

Jack Darby and William Du Bois admit to a critical rather than an analytical agenda, noting in the introduction to their gargantuan tome *American Film Music* that they were guided "more by the popular or critical success of a film than by the artistic merits of its music."[32] *Now, Voyager* is considered beside *Jezebel* and *Dark Victory*, and the authors do suggest that Steiner's aim in the scores for Bette Davis films was to explore the emotional dimensions of the narrative. In the chapter on Steiner, melodic themes in the scores are labelled with key words: Charlotte's theme is described as the "unhappy" theme, and the composer is accused of "artistic carelessness" in bringing the theme in after the opening credits and not establishing Charlotte's character evolution from the film's outset.[33] This suggests that the score somehow does not do justice to the film, although the authors are convinced that "the motivic approach of Korngold and Steiner is more in keeping with what film music should do and be."[34] Although it was published in 1990, the subjective, almost journalistic perspective of this text seems more contemporary to Steiner than to the modern film musicology to which it belongs: it highlights the diversity that exists in critical reception, and how differently the challenges of interpreting film music might be met.

Gorbman makes a very modern, psycho-sociological theorisation of Steiner's achievement in a particular scene, while Darby and Du Bois berate him for misusing the innate memorability of his melodies, creating a subtle, but significant shift in the way the composer is perceived: for Gorbman, the score is read as a package of intentions waiting to be unpacked in different ways; for Darby and Du Bois, a single reading of how a score should be constructed empowers a critical agenda for this particular text. The interpretation of film music can make it difficult to avoid a subjective perspective, particularly if the music is prized for its non-representational, gap-filling accessibility. Modern film musicology frequently evaluates scores for their success in manipulating the fantasy realm in the context of music's own valuable ambiguity, yet in the case of Steiner, this task is made much more difficult because he structured and labelled his scores in a *quasi* representational way, using established cultural and musical codes to make his objectives more explicit. Thus, although the consistencies in Steiner's scoring practice make it easy for us to appreciate his thematic designs and the significance of his diatonic-chromatic contrasts, even his insistence on waltzes and marches, on strings against woodwinds, make it clear that he was perpetuating the 'conspiracy' of composers to enjoy the indefinability of musical expression and experience. It is this which has allowed the discourses of film's linguistic parameters to celebrate their precision at the expense of music's proper place in narrative theories of film. Yet *Now, Voyager*, perhaps more than most films, invites us to relish both the ubiquity and understatement of Steiner's most lavish of scores.

Chapter 5

AN ANALYSIS OF THE SCORE

INTRODUCTION

Choosing a rationale for an analysis of this score, and more generally of Steiner's music, can be complicated. An analysis which focuses only on the development of melodic material would misrepresent a large proportion of the music in the film, yet to suggest that the score can be analysed entirely on the basis of its melodic construction would be superficial. It is also possible to explore Steiner's schemes of orchestration and his choices of instrumentation as encoding readings of romance, power and emotional instability, yet the orchestral choices lack significance without the formal context of the melodic and harmonic material which they colour. As theorists and critics have commented, Steiner wears his heart on his sleeve, he uses music unashamedly to express the drama, yet to view the score principally as a reaction to the other narrative elements is to ignore the coherence that it has in its own right. Taken out of its filmic context, the music can at times seem fragmented, changeable and unable to stand on its own, yet the repetition and development of various melodic ideas is clearly purposeful and directed.

The premise for this analysis reflects the varied aspects which characterise Steiner's music but ultimately explores what Steiner believed music could do for film: the interpretation and expression of the other narrative elements. His 'intellectualisation' of the story in musical structures, signalling and labelling characters, locales and emotional experiences, consistently underpins the role he gives to music, and it is on this basis that the analysis has been conceived. The themes of the score, and their developments and applications, will be labelled and discussed, as will those melodies which occur only once. This analysis does focus on the music as melody, but melody which is supported and characterised by orchestration and harmonic language. Melody was, for Steiner, the principal means of expression, and though such means seem clichéd by contemporary standards, his gift for such expression is fundamental to his conception of music's function in film. This analysis will not follow the chronology of the film beyond the evolutions of each individual theme: such a scheme would emphasise only the consistently reactive nature of the score and its capacity for storytelling. Instead the analysis will emphasise the strong internal coherence of the score and the relationships which exist between themes, as well as the potential for insight and interpretation which the music realises.

THEMES AND MELODIES

The term 'theme' has been commonly used in film musicology to define a musical idea which, through repetition, becomes associated with a particular element of the film, such as a character, place or dramatic event. These musical ideas are often melodic, but may also be primarily instrumental, harmonic or textural. Kathryn Kalinak suggests that the origins of this approach can be found in the "affinity . . . between Wagnerian opera and silent film" and their common use of leitmotivs to bring coherence to complex scores.[1] Claudia Gorbman emphasises that a theme can "accumulate meaning" by responding to nuances and small changes in the narrative context in which it is used, thus evolving beside the character or idea which it represents.[2] A composer may also use melodic ideas which capture or reflect the mood of a scene but, because they are not repeated again in the score, do not take on further narrative significance. In *Now, Voyager*, Steiner has used melodic material in both developed (thematic) and undeveloped forms, and the initial organisation of the analysis explores this difference in function. Labels given to themes and melodies in this analysis are entirely the choice of the author: Steiner gave no titles to the thematic ideas in the score for *Now, Voyager*, although he did label material in other scores, for example *The Oklahoma Kid* (1939) and *The Gay Sisters* (1942).[3]

Themes

The themes in the score for *Now, Voyager* are presented in the following order, and for this analysis they have been subtitled according to their locations in the film: the main title or 'voyager' theme, Charlotte's theme, Dr. Jaquith's theme, Tina's theme, the expectation theme, Jerry and Charlotte's theme or the love theme, Mrs. Vale's theme.

The main title music for the film, labelled for this analysis as the voyager theme, is a striking, expansive idea, characterised by a melody and countermelody construction. The melody is played across three octaves of strings and is balanced and contrasted by the simpler countermelody for French horns, celli and trumpet. The contrasts in rhythm and contour between the two motifs create a strong sense of motion through the theme as a whole and allow for significant variations in dynamic level. Title music has a responsibility for establishing the mood of the film, and Steiner's balance of chromatic/angular and diatonic/stepwise motion sets up the contrasts found between other themes in the film's score. The theme functions quite effectively in its role of opening the film: the pitch ranges of the instruments playing the melody lines dominate the soundscape, drawing the listener in immediately, and the small scale tension-resolution design of the theme creates a passionate and emotional feel to the music, signalling the drama of what is to follow.

Figure 5.1: Max Steiner, Voyager theme
Now, Voyager (1942) score, pp. 1-2.
Source: *Now, Voyager.* © M. Witmark & Sons, USA. Reproduced by
permission of IMP Ltd.

Charlotte's theme capitalises on the uncertainty generated by the chromatic
writing in the voyager theme, in the complexity of its harmony. The
combination of chords in the accompaniment, IV11 and ii6 in E major, gives a
major-minor duality, which is offset by the syncopation of the melody line. The
effect, particularly in conjunction with the visual images of Charlotte walking
down the stairs, is that the chords are dragging along behind the melody, giving
the anacrusian melody line a down-beat ambiguity. Overall, the theme has a
depressing quality, created by the falling contour of the melody line, which
seems constantly to be seeking resolution and rest on a note which fits with the
harmony. This is a particularly good example of how Steiner conceives of the
theme as a whole, rather than just the melody: the effect of the music is only
generated by the interaction between melody and accompaniment, and the theme
would be ineffective without the combination of both elements. As with the
voyager theme, Steiner uses partial repetition to extend the structure.

Figure 5.2: Max Steiner, Charlotte's theme
Now, Voyager score, pp. 13-14.
Source: *Now, Voyager.* © M. Witmark & Sons, USA. Reproduced by
permission of IMP Ltd.

Dr. Jaquith's theme shares many similarities with both the voyager theme and Charlotte's theme. The same mixture of anxiety and uncertainty as the voyager theme is evoked, but the progression from the chromatic to diatonic language reflects the path to psychological stability that Dr. Jaquith offers to his patients. The theme uses the repetition of short motifs found in both preceding themes, and the rhythmic suspensions give the melody line a sense of movement also heard before. The instrumentation for solo cello at the beginning of the melody line adds poignancy and weight to the theme, contrasting with the higher pitches of instruments used for Charlotte's theme to express her emotional fragility, such as violins, celeste and woodwind. The theme has a melodic contour which ascends over the full length of the statement, also contrasting it with Charlotte's theme.

Figure 5.3: Max Steiner, Dr. Jaquith's theme
Now, Voyager score, pp. 17-18.
Source: *Now, Voyager.* © M. Witmark & Sons, USA. Reproduced by
permission of IMP Ltd.

Tina's theme appears in the score long before she does: Steiner first employs the theme as Jerry shows Charlotte his family snapshot during the cruise. The theme then disappears until Charlotte sees Tina at Cascade, but in the first scene it provides a wistful quality to Jerry's description of his family. As soon as Charlotte sees Tina in the photograph she realises the connection between them, which is already implied by elements of Tina's theme. The falling contour of the melody line, the tension and resolution of the down-beat notes in the first two bars, evoke Charlotte's theme, but instead of the interminable descent, this theme concludes in pitch close to where it began. Steiner again employs small-scale repetitions, but the consequent restatement of the theme is begun a semitone higher, giving the melody a brighter context for its innate sadness.

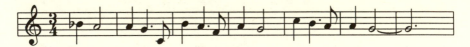

Figure 5.4: Max Steiner, Tina's theme
Now, Voyager score, pp. 73-74.
Source: *Now, Voyager.* © M. Witmark & Sons, USA. Reproduced by
permission of IMP Ltd.

The music which accompanies Jerry's gift of perfume to Charlotte, and her dressing for their dinner together, is used comparatively infrequently compared to the other themes, partly because it is a lengthy idea, constructed from a number of short motifs joined together: this detracts from its memorability and contrasts it with the simple designs of the other main themes. Its rapid semiquaver figures generate a strong sense of anticipation and excitement following Jerry's gift of perfume to Charlotte after their excursion, hence its subtitle of 'expectation' in this analysis. The repetition of the falling motif is balanced by the steadier ascending melody which uses the afterbeat rhythm of the Jaquith and voyager themes. Note how the variety of rhythmic motifs gives the music a sense of movement and energy: Steiner also marks it *poco agitato* and *appassionata*.

Figure 5.5: Max Steiner, Expectation theme
Now, Voyager **score, pp. 76-78.**
Source: *Now, Voyager.* © M. Witmark & Sons, USA. Reproduced by
permission of IMP Ltd.

The love theme also employs the lilting after-beat rhythm, but there is a clear diatonic contrast with the harmonic complexity of Charlotte's theme and a prevailing regularity of metre which gives stability.

Figure 5.6: Max Steiner, Love theme
Now, Voyager score, pp. 85-86.
Source: *Now, Voyager.* © M. Witmark & Sons, USA. Reproduced by
permission of IMP Ltd.

Again, the love theme uses small-scale repetitions and, as with Tina's theme, it is repeated higher after the first full statement. It is a more tonally stable theme than the others, but Steiner has created a bittersweet effect with the mixture of rising and falling contours.

Mrs. Vale's theme is the most diatonically and rhythmically stable of all the main themes in the score. The hint of military rhythm and the orchestration for brass give the theme a powerful feel, evoking Mrs. Vale's control over her family and her home. Again the theme is stated with repetition and ascending modulation.

Figure 5.7: Max Steiner, Mrs. Vale's theme
Now, Voyager score, p. 142.
Source: *Now, Voyager.* © M. Witmark & Sons, USA. Reproduced by
permission of IMP Ltd.

Melodies

Other melodic material which Steiner creates is for atmospheric purposes: the section of the film set on the cruise ship begins with an excursion, the music for which is a bright, energetic *allegretto*. It captures the enthusiasm of the purser, organising the travellers for their outing, though it does not reflect the rather surly individuals who are tired of waiting for Miss Beauchamp/Charlotte, nor the feelings of the anxious lady herself.

Figure 5.8: Max Steiner, Excursion melody
***Now, Voyager* score, p. 37.**
Source: *Now, Voyager*. © M. Witmark & Sons, USA. Reproduced by
permission of IMP Ltd.

For the lunchtime restaurant scene in Nassau, Jerry and Charlotte's first excursion together, Steiner has written some music for what he describes as a cafe orchestra. He gives very specific, perhaps rather extravagant instructions for the instrumentation: violin, guitar, tenor sax, three marimbas, one piano, one bass, one harp and timpani. He describes the tempo of the music as "Foxtrot (not fast)" and notes in the margin of the score: "I hear a screwy strange flavor—not necessarily oriental—we are in Nassau, where in reality there are only American jazz orchestras!"[4]

Figure 5.9: Max Steiner, Restaurant melody
Now, Voyager score, pp. 46-48.
Source: *Now, Voyager*. © M. Witmark & Sons, USA. Reproduced by
permission of IMP Ltd.

The repetition of the scalic melody on the marimbas and the continual drum
rhythms create a hypnotic tranquillity, which is contrasted by the wandering
triplet motif on the violin. The complete feel of the music is atmospheric, but its
lack of response to Charlotte's increasing anxiety in the scene makes her tension
seem even more apparent.

In the scene where Charlotte reveals her breakdown to Jerry, Steiner has
chosen to smooth the diegetic jazz band into a non-diegetic ensemble of similar
instruments, but with a less distinctive melodic character which does not distract
from the important dialogue of this scene. In the margin of the score he asks for
"A sort of 'Night and Day' idea—Romantic, not much figuration."[5] The melody
is unobtrusive and simple; note the similarity between the falling two-note motif
which begins the melody and the two-note motif which forms the basis for
Charlotte's theme. As the scene develops and Charlotte talks of her breakdown,
Steiner is able to bring in her theme without much disruption to the prevailing
melodic contour of the section.

Figure 5.10: Max Steiner, "Night and Day idea"
Now, Voyager **score, pp. 79-80.**
Source: *Now, Voyager.* © M. Witmark & Sons, USA. Reproduced by
permission of IMP Ltd.

The music Steiner has written for the mountain excursion functions in a
similar way to that which he wrote for the restaurant scene. Marked "Tempo di
Bolero (very rhythmic)," the music is very repetitive, and its continuity and
gradual ascending modulation provide additional tension to the increasing
nervousness of Jerry and Charlotte.[6] Again, Steiner has been very specific about
instrumentation, particularly the rhythmic qualities of the music, asking for half
the strings to be *pizzicato* and half *arco*, maracas, muffled side drums, timpani
and large tom-toms. The exotic atmosphere is conveyed through English horns,
alto saxophone and marimba. This material returns briefly in the montage in Rio
sequence.

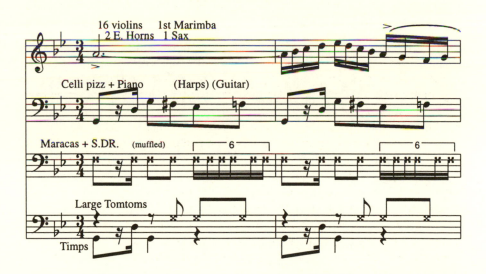

Figure 5.11: Max Steiner, Mountain Excursion melody
Now, Voyager score, pp. 92-93.
Source: *Now, Voyager.* © M. Witmark & Sons, USA. Reproduced by
permission of IMP Ltd.

The music for the tennis game, like that for the montage of the camping trip,
is both light and joyful. The former, *allegretto grazioso*, is orchestrated for
strings with bells and celeste; the latter, marked at the same tempo, is taken from
Steiner's score for *Four Daughters* (1938) and features similar orchestration.
There is also some continuity between the falling two-note motif in bar 9 of the
camping trip melody and the first two notes of Tina's theme, which accompanies
the scene which follows the montage.

Figure 5.12: Max Steiner, Tennis Game melody
Now, Voyager score, pp. 184-85.
Source: *Now, Voyager.* © M. Witmark & Sons, USA. Reproduced by
permission of IMP Ltd.

Figure 5.13: Max Steiner, Camping Trip Montage melody
***Now, Voyager* score, pp. 190-91.**
Source: *Now, Voyager*. © M. Witmark & Sons, USA. Reproduced by
permission of IMP Ltd.

There are also short fragments of music to express the hysteria and
emotional anxieties of both Charlotte and Tina. In the early scenes of the film
Steiner uses chromaticism, tremolo and fast rhythms to express the immediacy of
Charlotte's desperation when she is trapped in social situations with her mother
and Dr. Jaquith. This extract is from the first of these moments, when Mrs. Vale
reveals Jaquith as a psychiatrist to Charlotte.

Figure 5.14: Max Steiner, Charlotte's anxiety
Now, Voyager score, pp. 12-13.
Source: *Now, Voyager*. © M. Witmark & Sons, USA. Reproduced by
permission of IMP Ltd.

When Tina is having her nightmare at Cascade, Steiner expresses her
disorientation and emotional fragility using chromaticism, working on the
contrasts of falling mini-contours in a larger ascending line which characterise
Tina's original theme. The use of flute gives a very distinctive contrast to the
dominant string instrumentation of her theme.

Figure 5.15: Max Steiner, Tina's anxiety
Now, Voyager score, p. 177.
Source: *Now, Voyager*. © M. Witmark & Sons, USA. Reproduced by
permission of IMP Ltd.

Pre-composed Music

Most of the pre-composed music which is found in the soundtrack for *Now, Voyager* is drawn from popular songs of the 1930s: for example, Leeds and Dominguez's *Perfidia* for the Rio montage; Yellen and Friend's *You Belong to Me* in the ship's cocktail bar; Cole Porter's *Night and Day* for Charlotte and Jerry's reunion at Mrs. Weston's party. There is no cue-sheet available from the film's production, which would list the pre-composed numbers used, so it is not possible to be certain which of the songs were chosen by Steiner and which were suggested by scriptwriter Casey Robinson or producer Hal B. Wallis: Wallis was certainly fond of *Perfidia* and often included it in the diegetic soundtracks of his films, for example *Casablanca*. Steiner indicated in the score where the diegetic cues were to begin, and often sketched the first chord to indicate the key in which the music began. These cues were recorded in the studio, and other members of the Music Department were responsible for the arrangements, although Steiner clearly knew how they would sound in the context of his music: for example, he indicates the orchestration of *Perfidia*, which he calls "Rhumba," and gives the outline of the melody, so that the blending between this diegetic segment and the prevailing non-diegetic scoring of the montage is clear.[7] The other major quotation from pre-composed music is the concert performance of an extract from the first movement of Tchaikovsky's Sixth Symphony, which Charlotte attends with Elliot Livingston and Jerry. The significance of this music, which is used again in the last scene between Charlotte and Elliot, is discussed later in this chapter, but again Steiner gives an outline of the melody in the score to indicate how it will fit with the orchestration of the non-diegetic music which enters for the scene between Charlotte and Jerry at the rail station.

Motivic Coherence

An aspect of this score, which analysis of the written text can bring out more strongly than analysis of the aural text, is the similarity between motifs in different themes and melodies. For example, Steiner has used a form of suspension-resolution to characterise elements of many of the different themes and melodies in the score:

Figure 5.16a: Max Steiner, Charlotte's theme: 2-note motif
Now, Voyager **score, p. 13.**

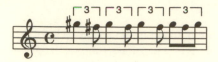

<table>
</table>

Figure 5.16b: Max Steiner,	**Figure 5.16c: Max Steiner,**
Expectation theme: repeated motif	**Tina's theme: opening**
***Now, Voyager* score, p. 77.**	***Now, Voyager* score, p. 73.**

Figure 5.16d: Max Steiner,	**Figure 5.16e: Max Steiner,**
Dr. Jaquith's theme: first phrase	**Voyager theme: opening**
***Now, Voyager* score, p. 17.**	***Now, Voyager* score, p. 1.**

Figure 5.16f: Max Steiner, "Night and	**Figure 5.16g: Max Steiner,**
Day idea": opening motif	**Love theme: opening**
***Now, Voyager* score, p. 79.**	***Now, Voyager* score, pp. 85-86.**

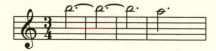

Figure 5.16h: Max Steiner, Love theme: ending
***Now, Voyager* score, p. 86.**

Steiner also used the rhythmic aspect of the suspension motif to propel melodies along energetically: the love theme gains great momentum from such a device. Furthermore, the themes below show consistency of design, not only with each other, but with the popular song *Perfidia*, used in the Rio de Janeiro montage sequence.

Figure 5.17a: Max Steiner, Steiner's sketch of "Rhumba" melody line (from Leeds and Dominguez's *Perfidia*) *Now, Voyager* score, p. 109.

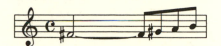

Figure 5.17b: Max Steiner, Expectation
theme: motif from beginning
Now, Voyager **score, p. 76.**

Figure 5.17c: Max Steiner, Expectation
theme: motif from middle
Now, Voyager **score, p. 77.**

Figure 5.17d: Max Steiner, Mountain Excursion melody: opening
Now, Voyager **score, p. 92.**
Source: *Now, Voyager.* © M. Witmark & Sons, USA. All figures reproduced by
permission of IMP Ltd.

THEMATIC EMPLOYMENT AND DEVELOPMENT

In contrast to many of his other scores, such as *They Died with Their Boots On* (1942) and *Mildred Pierce* (1945), Steiner seems to have under-developed much of the thematic material in this score. The principal themes of both these other scores are short and concise, offering and realising more potential for effective variation than can be found in the considerably more complex melodies which serve thematic purposes in *Now, Voyager*. In this score, however, Steiner has created a number of more subtle connections between thematic and melodic ideas, which become apparent during analysis and which contribute to the complete effect of the score.

Voyager, Charlotte, Dr. Jaquith, Mrs. Vale and the love themes are key stages in a score-wide strategy of harmonic suggestion, created by the relative presence of chromatic and diatonic language. The progression from the chromatic to diatonic across the five themes noted above, mirrors the emotional and psychological experiences of the film's main character, Charlotte, in a way which is more far-reaching than could have been achieved by the development of a single theme. The five themes are also connected by the passion which Charlotte experiences: its two extremes, its initial and ultimate incarnations, are represented by the voyager theme and the love theme. The three character-driven themes are framed by these extremes: Dr. Jaquith, whose psychological support unlocks the passion; Mrs. Vale, whose Puritanism represses it; Charlotte, who self-confessedly seeks it.

Voyager Theme

This framing of passion is established initially by the use of the voyager theme for the title sequence and its subsequent revival when Charlotte is first introduced visually. The very absence of a clear initial view of Charlotte, as we see only her hands and feet, places a great deal of responsibility on the music to provide insight and further detail about Charlotte in these early moments. In the scenes that follow, leading up to Charlotte's breakdown, Steiner alternates between Charlotte's own rather hesitant theme and the voyager theme, which between them quickly come to reflect the oppositional experiences which have characterised her life so far: her own theme for her repressed social confinement, the voyager theme for her liberated realisation of emotional and romantic ambition. Steiner's statement of the opening of the voyager theme on solo cello, as we first see Charlotte's hands, seems a lonely *cri de coeur*, accentuated by the high register of the instrument; however, in the context of the action that follows, and Charlotte's revelations to Dr. Jaquith about the cruise accompanied by the voyager theme in a more fully fledged version, it becomes a stifled echo of passion lost.

This fragmentation of the voyager theme is, in fact, not the first of the score, despite its proximity to the film's opening. At the end of the title sequence, as the credits fade into the opening scene, a maid is seen scuttling down the stairs in anticipation of Mrs. Vale's arrival. Steiner lifts a four-note descending motif from the countermelody to the voyager theme, repeating it sequentially to mickey-mouse the rapid steps of the maid's descent down the stairs.

Figure 5.18a: Max Steiner, Voyager theme countermelody
Now, Voyager score, p. 2.
Source: *Now, Voyager*. © M. Witmark & Sons, USA. Reproduced by
permission of IMP Ltd.

Figure 5.18b: Max Steiner, Descending Stairs motif
Now, Voyager score, p. 4.
Source: *Now, Voyager*. © M. Witmark & Sons, USA. Reproduced by
permission of IMP Ltd.

This captures the first moments of action, immediately imprinting Steiner's intentions for the score from the outset and forging a connection between the title music and the rest of the score. The simplicity and inanity of this motif and its function provide an ironic contrast to the depths of meaning and ambiguity of the cello motif used only minutes later. Such diversity from one theme is typical of

Steiner's pursuit of thematic significance.

Steiner uses the voyager theme to create a link between Charlotte's real and secret lives. His brief, mournful quotation of the theme's opening, when she is first shown in her bedroom—hands only, carving the ivory box, stubbing out the cigarette, wiping off the lipstick—has none of its original passionate resonance. He returns to the theme when Charlotte shows Dr. Jaquith her room, using it for much of the scene. The 'otherness' of this space to Charlotte, its security and privacy, is alluded to by both Charlotte herself, when she unlocks the door, and Dr. Jaquith, when he describes it as her castle. But Charlotte soon finds her secret life is not adequately hidden, as Jaquith sees the cigarette ends in the wastebin. Steiner sounds the voyager opening motif like a warning of marcato crotchets for violas and cellos, which is then strengthened, as Charlotte decides to brave it out with her scrapbook, by the same motif repeated by brass instruments. The fragmentation of the motif, the incompleteness of the original theme evoke Charlotte's desperation and her distance from her "secret life."[8] Only as the flashback begins does the voyager theme become stated more completely, with the high violins and full orchestration of the opening titles, and none of the darker anguish of Charlotte's confessional statement of mind. As the younger Charlotte and her lover, Leslie, kiss, Steiner introduces a new idea, which is an extension of the voyager countermelody. As with the short transitional motif at the very beginning of the film, the focus of the material is the four-note falling motif, but in this context Steiner uses chromatic stepwise motion to evoke the passion of the voyager theme but in a more compact melodic design.

Figure 5.19: Max Steiner, Voyager theme countermelody extension
Now, Voyager score, pp. 23-24.
Source: *Now, Voyager.* © M. Witmark & Sons, USA. Reproduced by
permission of IMP Ltd.

This secondary theme returns, marked *appassionata*, when Charlotte and Leslie are discovered in the car, and Steiner creates an incisive contrast in his own scoring, with violins, when Charlotte's voice over cuts through to the past: "I had said I was glad—and I *was* glad. He had defied my mother and placed me on a throne. . . . It was the proudest moment of my life!"[9]

Steiner also creates a more demure version of the main voyager motif as Charlotte's voice-over describes how they had to be discreet: the same melodic design, but none of the chromatic passion.

Figure 5.20: Max Steiner, Diatonic Voyager theme
Now, Voyager score, p. 27.
Source: *Now, Voyager*. © M. Witmark & Sons, USA. Reproduced by
permission of IMP Ltd.

Steiner also uses a fragment of the voyager motif to create a quirky, dissonant
texture for some commentary by Mrs. Vale on Charlotte's behaviour during the
cruise. Two flutes and an oboe perform a distinctive spiralling melody, re-used
as Charlotte recalls her mother's comments during her first meeting with Jerry.

Figure 5.21: Max Steiner, Flashback motif
Now, Voyager score, p. 25.
Source: *Now, Voyager*. © M. Witmark & Sons, USA. Reproduced by
permission of IMP Ltd.

The connection between the voyager theme and Charlotte's theme becomes
more apparent in the context of this flashback scene: the passionate chromaticism
and angular contour of the voyager theme are distilled into the ambiguous
harmony and dragging rhythm of Charlotte's theme, just as her current domestic
situation is a repressed echo of her youthful independence. At the beginning of
the film, Charlotte looks back on her past as the lost independence of youth,
symbolised narratively by the events on the cruise liner with Leslie and musically
by the voyager theme. Following her second cruise, with Jerry, and her
psychological reversal, the past with which Charlotte becomes more immediately
pre-occupied is her emotional instability and nervous breakdown. There are
many references to the breakdown in the dialogue and camera work, and
musically this becomes embodied by the use of Charlotte's theme, for much of
the film until she meets Tina. So the first stage of the musical evolution is
established: the passion of the voyager theme becomes overtaken by Charlotte's
theme, as Charlotte begins to move forward with her life.

Charlotte's Theme

The Breakdown. The first statement of Charlotte's theme is complicit with
the dialogue and camera work of the scene. We have still not been shown

Charlotte's face; instead we see only her feet dragging down the stairs towards the tea with her mother, whose voice is heard outlining her views of her daughter's lifestyle. Each component element of the narrative tells us something about Charlotte from a different point of view, and, at first hearing, the music seems only to mickey-mouse the rhythm of Charlotte's dread-full tread down the stairs. Closer inspection of the theme in its first version reveals, however, that the cross-rhythms are compounded by the harmonic complexity, making the theme seem 'out-of-synchronisation' with itself. This reflects Charlotte's sense of dislocation with the world she lives in, rather than the stability conveyed by her mother's terse summary. Charlotte is clearly unwilling to meet her mother for tea, but the instability of the theme implies a far greater internal tension in Charlotte's life than mere opposition to her mother.

Steiner introduces a variation of the theme when Charlotte is first seen at Cascade: again, the camera focuses on her hands first, but as Steiner notes in the score, "she is cured now."[10]

Figure 5.22: Max Steiner, 'Cured' version of Charlotte's theme
Now, Voyager **score, p. 35.**
Source: *Now, Voyager*. © M. Witmark & Sons, USA. Reproduced by
permission of IMP Ltd.

This statement of the theme is harmonically warmer than its predecessor: the change is created in the harmony of the chordal accompaniment from the combination of I9 - vi#6 to I6 - IV6; the bass line also drops by a fifth instead of a minor third. This scene clearly mirrors our first meeting with Charlotte—this time she is weaving instead of carving—but Steiner indicates Charlotte's progression in terms of the thematic scheme of the film, replacing the anxious voyager motif with Charlotte's own, minimally developed theme.

As Charlotte begins to become more self-confident, Steiner begins to break down the use of her theme into shorter statements, often juxtaposed and interwoven with other thematic ideas. This is partly a consequence of his particular use of music, catching frequent changes in the narrative with a sequence of different motifs to match, but, overall, the use of Charlotte's theme reflects the abatement of her self-obsession under the challenge of interest from and in other characters. Steiner's most effective employment of her theme is to give insight into the significance to Charlotte of some small piece of action.

A good example of this is her first appearance on the cruise, with her new glamorous image. The camera work again mirrors an earlier scene, beginning the shot with Charlotte's feet on the gangway as it did on the stairs at home, but this time the camera pans up her body. The audience quickly realises that this is a glamorous woman, although the transformation is so substantial that it may take a moment to recognise that this is still Charlotte. Steiner's placement of her theme here may have a signposting function to label this beauty as Charlotte, but what it also does is to remind us that behind the gloss and sophistication is the same insecure woman, at odds with her environment. Her social dislocation is far more apparent in the scenes that follow—her inability to match the loquacity of the ship's steward or to manage Jerry's enthusiasm—yet Steiner only uses the theme very briefly in this scene, just to catch her walking down the gangplank and to establish her experience. Its consequent absence emphasises quite poignantly how strange she finds her social context, an idea asserted more effectively by catching only the moment of her appearance with her theme, not the entire scene.

Another fleeting reminder of Charlotte's point of view is heard in the scene following the excursion as she returns to the ship with Jerry. He has been describing Tina, and Charlotte's recognition of herself in the child seems almost impolite and rather abrupt, although Jerry seems less surprised by the comment than Charlotte herself. Steiner, however, makes Charlotte's connection with Tina seem obvious and natural: he begins a short fragment of her theme on the same note that ends Tina's theme, creating continuity of pitch and melodic contour. Charlotte's theme has not been heard since she appeared on the gangplank, so its use here is deliberate and significant. Her anxiety over revealing her identity and the suppression of herself in her circumstances has caused her much social discomfort, and the real Charlotte Vale has not been glimpsed for some time. Jerry's quite casual remarks about his daughter unlock Charlotte's concealment of herself, and Steiner catches this immediately, briefly and without great drama. The statement is marked *Triste* in the score, and its orchestration of solo viola and cello on the melody, with accompaniment by harps, vibraphones and pianos, is simple but evocative.

Steiner's use of Charlotte's theme following her 'date' with Jerry in the cocktail bar serves as an effective contrast to its use in the excursion scene. In this scene the action has moved from an interior context, complete with diegetic jazz orchestra, to an exterior location on the ship's deck. The jazz orchestra can still be heard, though more faintly, and with the change in the song being played, Steiner uses the opportunity to move from diegetic to non-diegetic music. His "Night and Day idea" matches the contour of Charlotte's theme (figures 5.16f and 5.16a) which makes the transition from diegetic to non-diegetic, and from melodic to thematic, an effective yet unobtrusive one. Charlotte's theme, when finally heard, introduces and punctuates her description of her family. It evokes her personal sense of dislocation, doubly emphasised by Jerry's sequence of comments about the unusual qualities of the family members in the photograph. This is a long statement of the theme, repeated three times, modulating down by a major third after each statement. It comes to a halt as Charlotte identifies herself in the picture, the final admission needing no music to supplement it. Rather than describing the action, Steiner has used the theme to give an insight into Charlotte's emotional descent in this scene from social self-control to emotional unburdening. The theme falls as she does, and its neatness in the repeated modulating form highlights how effectively it can evoke spiralling depression.

Charlotte's theme is not heard again until the scene in the mountain cabin, where Charlotte and Jerry are spending the night after the accident. Steiner's statement of it here is only brief, and its function seems rather unusual when compared with earlier statements. Jerry, who has awoken in the night, leans over Charlotte to tuck the coat around her and kisses her gently. Instead of the continuation of the love theme, which has given coherence to the scene's ellipsis, the use of the second, warmer version of Charlotte's theme suggests Jerry's sympathy for Charlotte's vulnerability. Charlotte is asleep, and the theme does not seem to give insight to her feelings, but it does pre-empt Jerry's confession to her in the scene which follows, that since she confessed her breakdown to him he cannot get her out of his mind.

Return to Boston. As Charlotte's relationship with Jerry escalates, the narrative function of her theme becomes obsolete, but once Charlotte returns to Boston to face her old life and to try to live her new one, Steiner revives her theme. He uses quite small variations to reflect the broad palette of emotional experiences she is having, yet they represent quite accurately the difficulty of Charlotte's engagements with her mother. The staircases in the Vale house are used frequently in the scenes which follow, as they were at the film's opening, to suggest the distance between Charlotte and her mother; the different floors on which the two characters occupy rooms, connected by staircases, symbolise their different positions. The two chords which are heard as Charlotte approaches the front door sound like metaphorical door chimes: they not only reintroduce Charlotte to the house, but also herald the return of the original statement of her theme played an octave higher than usual. It is orchestrated, as Steiner describes it, "stringy, mit harps, celeste and Vibra,"[11] giving quite a warm effect despite the high register. Charlotte walks up the stairs towards her mother's room with the nurse, Dora, creating clear parallels with the opening statement of Charlotte's theme. Unlike this earlier occasion, the falling contour of the music does not emphasise Charlotte's depressive character, but instead evokes the heavy weight of memories which Charlotte must drag around on return to the house. As she ascends the stairs, Steiner creates an elegant counterpoint in the music: the statement of the theme, with modulations and repeats, falls almost an octave and a half in pitch from beginning to end.

The confrontation with her mother proves as awful as Charlotte expects it to be, despite her efforts to be cheerful, and as she leaves the room Steiner repeats the very first statement of her theme in the original key and pitch. Charlotte is again on the move, but the sound of her high-heeled shoes on the wooden floor is slow, and Steiner has deliberately not attempted to match their rhythm with that of the theme. Steiner connects three statements of the theme together, falling a major third each time, again giving the sense of descent into gloom. Then, as the maid, Hilda, appears with the box, revealed to contain a corsage of camellias from Jerry, the mood is immediately lifted by sequence of "ethereal" chords for celeste, harps, flutes, clarinets and vibraphone, which ascend in stepwise pairs.[12]

Figure 5.23: Max Steiner, Ascending chord sequence
Now, Voyager **score, p. 127.**
Source: *Now, Voyager.* © M. Witmark & Sons, USA. Reproduced by
permission of IMP Ltd.

Again, as Charlotte's spirits pick up, the narrative role for her theme is diminished, but just as the battle between Charlotte and her mother is enacted in stages, so her theme will return to reflect the difficulties of the engagement. As Mrs. Vale reminds Charlotte of the "recompense for having a late child," Steiner reminds us that this is blackmail which will hit Charlotte hard, again using the first statement of her theme a semitone lower, and marking it "Slow and Heavy."[13] Its perpetual descent, again modulating down by three consecutive major thirds, follows Mrs. Vale out to the staircase, down which she dramatically falls as her daughter's theme ends. By contrast, the use of Charlotte's theme at the close of the family party is warmly orchestrated for 16 violins and celeste, far less harmonically ambiguous, and arranged in a more stately 4/4 rhythm. Charlotte has settled difficulties with the rest of her family, particularly June, and they have begun to accept her new look and personality.

Figure 5.24: Max Steiner, 4/4 version of Charlotte's theme
Now, Voyager **score, p. 138.**
Source: *Now, Voyager.* © M. Witmark & Sons, USA. Reproduced by
permission of IMP Ltd.

As Charlotte mounts the stairs to face another interview with her mother, who has not begun to accept her new image, Steiner reverts to the original rhythms and harmonies of the theme, reverting to the sombre timbres of horns and cor anglais and a lower pitch.

The crucial conversation between Charlotte and her mother that follows is unscored while they fence around each other, casting occasional challenges forth. However, as soon as Charlotte reveals the real change in herself, that she is not afraid of her mother any more, Steiner introduces music, notably Charlotte's own theme. It cuts through the silent tension of the dialogue, a revelation to Charlotte herself, the high pitch and gentle timbre of the violins, vibraphone and celeste like an ethereal inner strength. This very brief statement of the theme seems to quash her anxieties with her mother for good, as the theme is not heard again while Mrs. Vale is still alive. Steiner only hints briefly at the essence of the theme immediately after Mrs. Vale's heart attack, descending a slow chromatic scale step-by-step as Charlotte confesses their quarrel to the nurse: the descending line is a shadow of Charlotte's theme, just as she finds her strength suddenly repressed by the enormity of the event.

New Ties. With Charlotte's old ties finally broken, Steiner reminds us of the new ones when she returns to Cascade and meets Tina. Charlotte reveals first sympathy, then empathy to Tina, both when they first meet and later when she is telling Tina a story to help her sleep. In this first instance, Steiner echoes Charlotte's theme with solo violin, viola, vibraphone, harp and celeste, broadening out to a fuller warmer orchestration as Tina becomes less hostile. As Charlotte admits to being reminded of herself, Steiner shifts from the 6/8 to 4/4 versions of the theme, removing the cross-rhythms provided by the accompaniment line: the lack of rhythmic instability reflects Charlotte's greater ease with herself. Later that night, as Charlotte tries to comfort the child, her theme becomes rather shimmery, the celeste and vibraphone creating an effect Steiner describes as "Ethereal—eine reminiscence!"[14]

While Charlotte is happy to share experiences with Tina, she wishes to keep her identity concealed from Jerry when Tina first calls him from the cafe. She sees an opportunity to get to know Tina without the added complication of her relationship with Jerry, and Steiner's use of Charlotte's theme here, rather than the love theme, suggests that she wants to keep the relationships separate for now. Furthermore, even though Charlotte is happy to admit that Jerry was there for her when she needed someone, she is still ultimately alone, and it is this ability to accommodate solitude that she is trying to help Tina with. Steiner's ear for a *double entendre* is well employed here as he repeats the statement of Charlotte's theme from the mountain cabin scene: just as the events of that night have been kept secret from everyone, so Charlotte now asks Tina to keep her identity a secret from Jerry.

As Tina begins to heal her emotional scars, Charlotte's theme once again ceases to have pro-active narrative significance, and becomes only recollective. It is used as Charlotte lists the names that Tina might call her by, names which represent Charlotte's own emotional evolution. Steiner marks the score "Triste" here, although this is more a reflective than a sad moment in the narrative. It is also used during the final dialogue between Charlotte and Jerry, when he asks her why she did not marry Elliot Livingston. Steiner quotes Charlotte's theme just as it was used in her first meeting with Elliot, in its 4/4 metre. It is a brief recollection of the past: Jerry recalls a part of Charlotte's life he does not understand; Charlotte recalls the new found confidence she displayed that evening. It is only a brief quotation, but it is a fittingly ambiguous final statement of a theme which has represented emotional instability, memory and insecurity. The varied form of the theme, reflecting two perceptions of the same person, evokes the uncertainty of emotional experience, but its brief and transitory statement suggests that this person is in the past, if not forgotten.

Dr. Jaquith's Theme

Dr. Jaquith's theme is often heard in juxtaposition with Charlotte's theme or the voyager theme, which implies that it might most easily be appreciated in relation to them. Certainly in the opening scenes of the film, when Charlotte and Dr. Jaquith are becoming acquainted, his theme is juxtaposed against them as he shows interest in Charlotte's carving and later tries to offer consolation as she cries. Little development or alteration occurs in subsequent use of the theme, but what Steiner does most effectively is to use orchestration to match the theme to other contextual thematic statements, just as Jaquith matches his demeanour to that of his patients. This begins when Jaquith is examining Charlotte's carvings: the solo cello introduces his theme just as it had introduced us to Charlotte through the voyager motif. Jaquith is expressing warm admiration to Charlotte of her handiwork, and the string instrumentation and medium range of the solo cello emphasise his mood and do much to ameliorate the melodic quirkiness created by the chromaticism.

Following Jaquith's succinct announcement of Charlotte's breakdown to Mrs. Vale, Steiner repeats Jaquith's theme to announce the change in location to the sanatorium, Cascade. Here, on his own territory, Jaquith is energetic, bullish and bright: his theme gains strength from a faster tempo and brightness from a fuller orchestration with the melody carried by violins, and horns, cellos and violas on the countermelody. The next ellipsis in time and place is also managed by Jaquith's theme, as Charlotte reflects on the Walt Whitman quotation Jaquith has given her: "Untold want, by life and land ne'er granted, Now, voyager, sail thou forth to seek and find." As the image of the cruise ship is faded in, Steiner opts for a lower, sonorous orchestration of French horns, saxophones, violas and cellos, echoing the ship's horn, with a supplementary aquatic feel created by tremolo violins and rippling harps.

This statement of the theme begins a long musical cue lasting about 15 minutes, which extends through the excursion to the deck scene between Charlotte and Deb McIntyre. Jaquith's theme is slotted in to catch a relevant piece of action, the brief flashback to his advice to Charlotte about taking part. This flashback is one of two, which together remind us of the contrasting influences Jaquith and Mrs. Vale have on Charlotte's life. Both flashbacks are accompanied by appropriate thematic statements, blurred into the main musical texture by rippling harps. Both musical fragments are also orchestrated at high pitch, matching the harps, although contrasting instrumentation is used: the opening of Jaquith's theme is heard on shimmering tremolo violins; the quirky, dissonant voyager motif (figure 5.1) uses flutes and oboe. Jaquith's motif sounds distinctly less threatening, less obtrusive, and Charlotte's response to recalling his advice is calm and measured, in contrast to her barbed reaction to thoughts of her mother.

Jaquith's theme is not heard again while Charlotte becomes more confident and finds comfort in her relationship with Jerry, its muteness comparable with that of Charlotte's own theme. Its return is unusual, in its juxtaposition with the love theme during the romantic climax of this part of the film, the balcony scene. The low volume renders the theme rather inconspicuous, despite the repeat of the original orchestration for cello, yet Steiner's choice and placement of Jaquith's theme in this scene are quite deliberate. The score indicates that the theme is to begin precisely as Charlotte remarks that she is immune to happiness and is to end when Jerry proposes what he would do if he were free. Jaquith's theme responds to a psychological subtext in the dialogue at this point: much was made in contemporary reviews of the film of the psychological and psychiatric aspects to the film's story. Steiner could have scored this scene quite simply and more consistently with the love theme alone, but the dialogue here does consider issues of state of mind and emotional experience, in a way that much of the rest of the film, even Charlotte's conversations with her psychiatrist, does not. The rapid-fire exchange of one-liners between Jerry and Charlotte makes this far from a heavyweight emotional soliloquy, yet Jaquith's theme highlights that Charlotte's happiness is the goal of her psychological journey, and its register contrasts with the pitching of the love theme, further emphasising its subtextual significance.

Once Charlotte has returned to Boston, Jaquith's influence is muted at first. Even though his voice is recalled in her mind as she prepares to meet her mother again, Steiner does not use his theme, preferring instead the dissonant voyager motif to reflect the anticipation of conflict with her mother.[15] Once Charlotte has settled the relationship with her mother for herself, Jaquith's theme does return to accompany the letter writing episode: the scene acts as a narrative device to explain the progress in the relationship between Elliot and Charlotte, but it also begins to establish Charlotte and Jaquith as more equal than patient-doctor. The measured tones of Charlotte's voice-over and Dr. Jaquith's bemused but passive response are both matched by the steady tempo and middle pitch of Jaquith's theme which accompanies the scene: his influence over her life is still present, but she is beginning to determine her own destiny. Steiner orchestrates both melody and countermelody with strings, removing the usual contrast between the motifs, and brings in a solo violin as Charlotte talks about Elliot's proposal. He then borrows this implied romance as he extends the statement of Jaquith's theme into the next scene, where Charlotte is arranging her roses, delaying the final cadence until Mrs. Vale describes Elliot as a feather in the Vale family cap.

This overlap lessens the potential narrative fragmentation in the Charlotte-Elliot relationship between the letter scene and the conversation with Elliot about marriage, but it also seems to be an unusual intrusion on the established silence that has characterised most conversations between Charlotte and her mother.

Charlotte's chance of emotional breakdown over the death of her mother is resonated by Jaquith's theme during the scenes which immediately follow the fatal row between Charlotte and her mother. The rising chromatic figuration that accompanies Charlotte's desperate retaliation to her mother's accusations and the steady, sorrowful chromatic downstepping which mark her relenting both borrow from the chromatic elements in Jaquith's theme. Later his theme comes to the rescue more directly, in an almost exact repeat of the first visit to Cascade: Charlotte's emotional homecoming is marked by warm and sedate strings and a restful cadence after the juxtaposition of a number of different thematic motifs over a sequence of short scenes. Steiner echoes Jaquith's influence from a distance as Charlotte admits that her return to Cascade has worked another miracle, the solo cello evoking the first statement of his theme, although subtextually Charlotte is learning to heal herself by focusing on someone else's troubles, namely Tina's.

The equilibrium between Jaquith's guidance and Charlotte's self-directed journey towards emotional stability finds its resolution in the scene where they confront each other about Tina. The balance of views expressed in this dialogue, the exchange of power and decision-making responsibility shows how far Charlotte has grown and how healthy she has become. Steiner matches this equilibrium with silence, illustrating that their relationship has moved beyond Charlotte's introspection or Dr. Jaquith's way forward. This is mirrored in the last scenes at the Vale house, when Charlotte and Jaquith are discussing the extension to Cascade Charlotte has paid for and her involvement in the sanatorium. There is background diegetic music from a gramophone, and its happy dance rhythms counterpoint the intimacy and equality of the conversation between Charlotte and Jaquith.

Jaquith's presence in Charlotte's and Tina's recuperations is hinted at during the camping montage. Tina is cooking potatoes on the fire, and Charlotte emerges from the tent with a letter for Dr. Jaquith requesting that Tina return to Boston with her. Steiner creates a short repeated fragment, which keeps the jolly mood of the camping sequence but clearly refers to Jaquith's theme (figure 5.3).

Figure 5.25: Max Steiner, repeated motif from Camping Trip Montage
***Now, Voyager* score, p. 193.**
Source: *Now, Voyager*. © M. Witmark & Sons, USA. Reproduced by
permission of IMP Ltd.

It also imitates the first section of music used for the montage, borrowed from Steiner's score for *Four Daughters* (1939) (figure 5.13), and the middle motif of the expectation theme (figures 5.5 and 5.17c).

Ultimately, however, Dr. Jaquith remains the powerful influence in Charlotte's life, of which we are reminded in the film's final scene between Charlotte and Jerry. Charlotte admits that Jaquith knows of the affair and explains that his wisdom of what is best for Tina now restrains any resumption of affection between her and Jerry. The theme is richly orchestrated for strings, in keeping with the instruments which are sounding out the contextual statements of the love theme. Jaquith's theme retains its ascendant qualities, giving a sense of hope at a tense and desperate cross-roads in the direction of the relationship between the lovers. The theme only begins to fall as Charlotte announces that she might lose Tina and pleads with Jerry for help.

It is to Steiner's credit that he has chosen not simply to express Jaquith as a simple characterisation, but to incorporate his theme into the chromatic-diatonic progression to evoke this emotional aspect of the story and its psychological twist. Jaquith's professional dabbling in emotions and his judgmental position on the course of narrative events make him a powerful figure, and the employment, and occasional circumventing, of his theme give a careful musical expression of these issues. Above all, Jaquith's theme combines hope with an understanding of the dissonance of emotional breakdown, and it provides an important contrast to Charlotte's theme, particularly in the first half of the score.

The Love Theme

Expectation and Romance. For logical narrative reasons, the love theme only appears after the first forty-five minutes of the film, although it is not the last of the major themes to be introduced. There is preparation for the theme, however, in the expectation theme (figure 5.5), which suggests the potential for intimacy and understanding between Charlotte and Jerry. Both these themes are characterised by their diatonic character, with scalic and triadic melodic design and uncomplicated harmonic progressions. This contrasts them with both Charlotte's and Jaquith's themes, but in the context of the film's story progression it also establishes them, particularly the love theme, as a musical expression of Charlotte's narrative goal. This is further accentuated by the suspensions and accented neighbour notes in the love theme and the triplet suspension-resolution motif in the expectation theme (see figures 5.16h. 5.16g, and 5.16b respectively).

The first indication of intimacy between Jerry and Charlotte is found in the scene where they return to the ship from their excursion. The expectation theme catches Jerry's change in mood from talking about his daughter to giving Charlotte the perfume: Steiner lifts the timbre by removing mutes from the strings after the brief statement of Charlotte's theme and the tempo is pushed forward. The change in tempo, the breadth of pitch range covered by the melody and accompanying motifs, and the faster rhythms of the semiquavers all suggest an element of emotional abandon and unpredictability; though each motif is quite directional, the patchwork effect of the theme as a whole catches Charlotte's anticipation of her evening date very effectively.   In her dressing-for-dinner scene, where she mutters in an undertone about shoes and bags, her eagerness to do the right thing is the first expression of feeling we have seen from her since her breakdown.   Steiner repeats a section of the theme for this scene, adding small bells and marking *appassionata* and *crescendo* into the score.   Steiner builds the tension of this moment alone with Charlotte by juxtaposing the suspension resolution motif (figure 5.16b) with glissandi harps ascending and descending in each bar.

The function of the expectation theme becomes quite apparent when the score is looked at more generally. The music of the first two narrative locations, the Vale house and Cascade, is predominantly chromatic, particularly when compared with the music of the cruise. Although Steiner's thematic interjections of Charlotte's and Jaquith's themes are essentially narratively driven, they also collude with the restaurant music to convey Charlotte's feeling of uneasiness about the cruise. Nevertheless, the expectation theme clearly signals a prevailing change of mood in the context of the music which follows: the bright foxtrot and the love theme. Even though Charlotte's theme is heard during the deck scene, it now seems the odd theme out in the brighter, warmer, more diatonic musical landscape which has been introduced in response to Jerry's interest in Charlotte. Nonetheless, Steiner takes no chances in the presentation of the love theme, using a pause in the music to allow Jerry's "Feeling better?" and Charlotte's "Much" to signal the next stage in their intimacy. These are small beginnings for the romance, and Steiner is simple in his orchestration, just 16 violins divisi and celeste for the first seven bars, joined only as the melody reaches its conclusion by muted violas and cellos. Although it is in 3/4, he marks it to be played as if in one, leaving rhythmic feeling to be provided by *rubato* and by the afterbeat and upbeat movement. Steiner emphasises the more positive mood of this part of the film, and of the theme, by a modulation up by a minor third for the second statement of the theme, perhaps a subtle reference to Charlotte's very personal admission, "I almost felt alive." As Charlotte and Jerry part, Steiner drops the pitch again, reverting from the initial *tempo di valse* to a heavier 12/8 metre, which is then combined most effectively with a minor harmonisation as Charlotte endures her night turmoils:

Figure 5.26: Max Steiner, 12/8 version of Love theme
***Now, Voyager* score, p. 88.**
Source: *Now, Voyager.* © M. Witmark & Sons, USA. Reproduced by
permission of IMP Ltd.

The conversation between Charlotte and Deb about Jerry's marriage is without music, and it is the first unscored segment of film since Charlotte meets Lisa at Cascade. Steiner refrains from musical comment about Jerry's situation until he and Charlotte are looking out over Rio harbour, resuming where he left off with the love theme in its minor mode, four beat version for solo cello and cor anglais, resuming at the same pitch and key. Perhaps it is Jerry's turn to feel anxiety, although Charlotte's arm-squeezing gesture of compassion again shows her emotionally, feelings exposed by Jerry and expressed with the love theme.

The balcony scene and the airport scene which follows are scored quite simply with the love theme, although Steiner employs broad ranges in dynamics, pitch and texture. During the balcony scene he also introduces an extension to the love theme, which has its own countermelody much like those of the voyager and Jaquith themes:

Figure 5.27: Max Steiner, Love theme extension
Now, Voyager **score, p. 112.**
Source: *Now, Voyager.* © M. Witmark & Sons, USA. Reproduced by permission of IMP Ltd.

This allows the love theme to have a fuller statement without continually repeating the four bar unit. The chromatic element of the violin motif contrasts effectively with the diatonic nature of the main love theme and introduces an element of extra passion. This underpins the tension in Jerry's conversation with Charlotte as he tries to express himself and draw more than cynicism from her. The instrumentation of the balcony scene is rich, with equal numbers of violins, violas and cellos employed, supplemented by vibraphone, chimes and harp, although Steiner seems unable to resist a symbol of unadulterated romance when he inserts the solo violin to support Jerry's declaration of what he would do if he were free. It is this approach to scoring romantic scenes which helped form a perception of Steiner as milking conventions of nineteenth-century Romantic

orchestral music; however, the use of celeste, piano and vibraphone gives a gloss
and sparkle to the sound to create a cliché that is essentially Steiner's own.

The balcony scene closes with a rare cadence, in C major, although Steiner
imposes an added sixth onto the tonic chord from the rather mournful cor anglais
and horn countermelody, a reminder of a jazz idiom and a mild portent of the
gloom which follows in the next scene. The airport farewell continues in the
12/8 metre which ended the balcony scene, but it introduces another variation on
the love theme, derived from its last phrase.

Figure 5.28: Max Steiner, Love theme variation
***Now, Voyager* score, p. 117.**
Source: *Now, Voyager.* © M. Witmàrk & Sons, USA. Reproduced by
permission of IMP Ltd.

Its ascending design is juxtaposed with the A minor key, connecting it
subtextually to the previous scene and perpetuating the bittersweet mood.
Steiner shifts motifs between instrumental groups and pitch registers, introducing
the more poignant effects of woodwind among the strings and generating a
fragmented feeling at the scene's opening. The return of the original love theme
is inevitable, although Steiner cannot resist squeezing emotion out of the music
as the lovers kiss, pushing out sudden crescendos and decrescendos to amplify
the passion. It is the least subtle gesture of the score, a resort to mickey-mousing
in the context of the prevailing intellectual conception of the themes. His next
gesture, the chromatic and orchestral shift as the camera cuts back to a pained-
looking Jerry watching Charlotte's plane leave, seems similarly awkward: the
hollow cor anglais, flute, bassoons and French horns are a dramatic contrast to
the lush, romantic strings, but the device seems simplistic in contrast to the more
subtle operations performed elsewhere in these scenes.

Love without Jerry. The love theme speaks for Jerry once Charlotte has
returned to Boston, its almost total absence from the score in this section of the

film reminding us that he has no place in her life now; as Charlotte herself puts it in the car with Elliot, "I have only a dried corsage and an empty bottle of perfume and I can't even say his name."[16] Even when the corsage of camellias arrives Steiner responds initially in spite of the conventions he established during the earlier love scenes: the tension of Charlotte opening the box of flowers is evoked by harps, flutes, clarinets, celeste and vibraphone, and Steiner specifically notes in the score, "no strings please."[17] When he brings the love theme in, it is exactly as it was first heard on the cruise ship, a literal echo of the past, and the delay of the final cadence of the theme as Charlotte is dressing for dinner hangs over her, protecting her from the imminent disapproval of her mother.

Steiner's definition of the love theme as stylistically romantic is highlighted by the introduction of a section of the first movement from Tchaikovsky's Sixth Symphony, the "Pathétique," to represent Charlotte's relationship with Elliot, and the choice she finds herself having to make is encapsulated by the juxtaposition of the two melodic ideas. It is clearly significant that Charlotte's relationship with Elliot has no original non-diegetic theme of its own, and also that Steiner borrows from the culturally constructed passion of the symphony to heighten the lack of intellectual, emotional or physical consummation that characterises their courting. Ironically, the empowerment of pre-composed music over the original, narrative-driven theme is initiated during the reunion of Charlotte and Jerry at Mrs. Weston's party, where their double talk of politeness and intimacy is underscored by a piano version of Cole Porter's *Night and Day*. The absence of lyrics in the song performance symbolises the lack of opportunity for the characters to express their feelings to one another: this is, quite literally, a song without words which, if they were heard, would represent the lovers' feelings perfectly. This is immediately followed by the dynamic and gushingly performed Tchaikovsky, which envelops Jerry, Charlotte and Elliot as they sit at the concert. Charlotte's commitment to Elliot prevails at this point, and she does not revive her romance with Jerry: throughout their conversation at the rail station Steiner only fragments the love theme into short phrases, or uses it in the minor, until their moment of understanding when he returns to a major tonality and a complete statement of the theme. This level of intimacy and comprehension is one which Elliot and Charlotte can never reach, and this inadequacy is symbolised by the radio performance of the Tchaikovsky movement. The diegetic pre-composed symphony represents the propriety of social conventions within which Elliot 'feels' for Charlotte; its second-hand reproduction, a diegesis within a diegesis, reinforces the awkwardness with which Charlotte's real desires and emotions sit against Elliot's 'romantic' expectations of her.

Just as Jerry is effectively absent from Charlotte's life in Boston, so he remains obscured when she returns to Cascade and meets Tina. Charlotte is anxious to become acquainted with Tina on her own terms, and the connection with Jerry is only realised musically when Charlotte accidentally calls the child

Tina, the name only Jerry uses. The recollection of the love theme is only faint, a very high solo violin and celeste, and does not intrude into Tina and Charlotte's important negotiations of friendship. The theme only imposes itself on their relationship when Jerry enters the family, near the end of the film when he comes to the Vale house to see Tina and Charlotte: as Jerry holds his daughter in his arms, he looks up to Charlotte and tells them both "I love you." Steiner uses the augmented fourth in the second phrase to add tension to the moment, and the second statement of the theme runs directly into Tina's theme: this allows the love between Jerry and Charlotte to surface only momentarily, before it is overtaken by the newest element in their relationship, Tina.

Steiner uses the love theme to punctuate and underpin Jerry and Charlotte's negotiations about the future of their relationship in the film's final scenes, creating a series of final stages on the road to understanding. Steiner first introduces music in the scene as Jerry abruptly changes the subject from Tina to his relationship with Charlotte.[18] Nevertheless, the use of the theme in this final scene reflects the progression in Charlotte's point of view, and Steiner seems to throw it out like a lifebelt as the empathy between Charlotte and Jerry struggles to survive. He begins by recalling the minor version of the theme which accompanied Charlotte's dash to the station to save the relationship the first time around. As Jerry begins to understand her point of view, Steiner retrieves the situation musically with a slow, major restatement of the theme: he is careful to play on the irony of suppressed passion in the faltering embrace by restating the theme without the usual ascendant modulation. As Jerry drops his head and walks away, Steiner does the same musically, repeating the opening phrase in a descending sequence; then finally an acceptance, an emotional equilibrium, is reached between Jerry and Charlotte, and as the cigarettes are lit, Steiner brings in the theme again for its last flourish. He states it *come sopra* the beginning of the balcony scene, moment of their ultimate intimacy, perpetuating the irony of this final scene where the physical intimacy remains unconsummated. Steiner marks the score "Slowly and mit Schmaltz" for the cigarette lighting, the intimation of passion apparent in the high violins and lush orchestration. The intensity of the moment passes and the pitch of the music drops, fragmented by the statement of the love theme counter-theme, as they look into the night. Charlotte sounds a hopeful note and Steiner responds with the restoration of original theme and pitch, building through repetition, dynamic and rising modulation to the final climactic statement after Charlotte's famous last line.

The use of the theme in this final scene is entirely reactive to each small progression in the dialogue between the lovers, and heard as music alone, without the film's action, it seems fragmented, repetitive and lacking a single direction until the last thirteen bars.[19] The score shows, however, that Steiner is consciously recalling statements of the theme from earlier sections of the score, making deliberate connections with other stages in the narrative, most notably Charlotte's dash to the station, at the beginning of the scene, and the airport farewell at the end. This implies very strongly that he viewed the score and the film as a whole, making connections in his conception of the theme and the way it should be used and re-used. As a result the original, unfragmented love theme is only fully stated in three keys, G, Bb and A majors, and it remains anchored to a narrow pitch and instrumental form. Where with Charlotte's theme he relies on the effect of the theme's harmonic and rhythmic qualities, the love theme is defined more by the contrast between complete and fragmented statements, major and minor keys, and strings and wind orchestrations which affect pitching. This creates a very striking identity for the theme, which achieves its own sense of closure and completeness with the dominance of high string orchestrations in the final moments of the film.

Tina's Theme

This theme is introduced when Jerry and Charlotte are returning from their first excursion together, and Jerry is describing his family. The 3/4 metre contrasts with the regular repetitive figures of the restaurant music, and though this new melody does not immediately have an obvious thematic function, it reflects Charlotte's more relaxed mood. This narrative expression is captured by the similarities between Charlotte's and Tina's theme in the use of falling two note motifs. Although the harmonic functions of the two motifs are understood slightly differently, the immediate effect is very similar, and Tina's theme seems to be a brighter version of Charlotte's. This relationship is reversed when the two characters finally meet at Cascade. Charlotte seems to be on the brink of another breakdown, but as soon as she sees Tina, she assumes a bright and comforting manner with the clearly depressed child.

Steiner articulates her recognition of Jerry's daughter with a comparatively rare example of signposting, waiting to begin the statement of Tina's theme until the camera gives Charlotte's own sight of her. The theme has a hesitant quality, as Charlotte debates whether to approach Tina, but soon resumes a steadier tempo as she assumes her friendly manner. Steiner matches the exchanges between the characters with the insertion of Charlotte's theme, particularly emphasising the similarity between the characters, but the prevailing mood in this scene is warm and optimistic, despite the falling contours of Tina's theme.

Steiner relies on variety in orchestration and tempo to colour his use of Tina's theme in the post-tennis scenes. When she calls her father a second time, the theme is introduced by a flamboyant ascending flourish of high violins, and the statement is fast and light as she gushes her news over the telephone. For the camping sequence Steiner segues the violin and high woodwind melody that opens the montage into Tina's theme, which begins fast and bright, but then slows down, dropping in timbre to violas and cellos, as the scene switches to night-time beneath the stars. As Charlotte invites Tina to return to Boston with her, the mood changes again to an uncomplicated violin orchestration, at middle pitch, as Tina explains how important Charlotte is to her. This is a scene of great intimacy, and Steiner adopts a childlike simplicity in conveying the significance of the action.

The instrumentation becomes lusher and more extravagant when the action returns to the glamorous interior of the Boston house. Tina calls her father's name, and Steiner uses the same device that marked the coins dropping in the phone box, with celeste and high wind and strings. As Tina comes down the stairs, Steiner marks her footsteps, as he once marked Charlotte's, using each note of Tina's theme for a different step.

Figure 5.29: Max Steiner, Tina's steps
***Now, Voyager* score, pp. 203-204.**
Source: *Now, Voyager*. © M. Witmark & Sons, USA. Reproduced by
permission of IMP Ltd.

Steiner sandwiches fragments of Tina's theme into the statements of the love theme which amplify the subtext of Charlotte and Jerry's reunion, and the theme is last heard as Tina disappears up the stairs with her father to show him her room. Steiner retains the high violins of the love theme, but ends Tina's theme with a perfect cadence, a happy-ever-after conclusion to her role in the narrative. Her life is complete, her father and adoptive mother share her love, and her world is decorated with new party dresses and a more confident self-image. The wrangling over how the adults around her will sustain this perfect world has still to be completed, but Steiner makes clear the closure of her emotional journey.

Mrs. Vale's Theme

Despite Mrs. Vale's dictatorial and unsympathetic greeting to Charlotte on her return, it is not until Charlotte deliberately flouts her mother's decisions that Steiner introduces music to express the formidable matriarch. There are a number of conversations between mother and daughter in this segment of the film, and Steiner has used music quite sparingly to make particular narrative statements. The theme is first heard when Mrs. Vale arrives to confront Charlotte about the flowers and her daughter's change of bedroom, and Steiner announces it with a pause in the expectation theme which precedes it. The held chord seems to underpin a momentary debate in Mrs. Vale's own mind about how critical to be of her daughter, but it becomes overtaken by the power and clear direction of Mrs. Vale's theme. She stands, upright and imperious, dictating her position, as her theme makes its point. The marcato quality is established from the outset, but Steiner leaves room for development in later statements by using only strings in the orchestration.

The scale of Mrs. Vale's power becomes much more apparent in her next confrontation with Charlotte where she announces the contents of her will. The scene has been unscored until Charlotte faces up to her mother's clear threat, a moment of courage brought out by Charlotte's theme. Steiner cuts straight across this theme with Mrs. Vale's own tune, rigid and rhythmic, at a contrasting lower pitch, orchestrated for brass. This regal music quite literally expresses Mrs. Vale's power, and the power she might pass on to Charlotte, the dotted rhythms conveying the orderly behaviour she expects Charlotte to adopt. Nurse Dora's appellation of Mrs. Vale as "Queen Elizabeth" seems an obvious source for Steiner's definition of the theme here, and the manipulation of the theme that follows this first statement is among the most carefully crafted that he wrote. As Mrs. Vale becomes sleepy from the hot toddy, the power seeps away from her: Steiner unwinds the orchestration from brass to brass and wind, wind and strings and finally strings alone, dropping the pitch of the theme at each stage.

The theme is heard only once more, when Mrs. Vale has died and the wreath is shown on the door. Steiner returns to brass, punctuated by bells, giving a sombre and evocative timbre in support of the minor key. The tempo is very slow, and the theme reaches its melodic peak as the lawyer announces that Charlotte has inherited everything. From here it descends in pitch and tension, and becomes more gently orchestrated for strings, picking up the tempo as the scene changes to the train. The theme seems to incorporate the rhythm of the train's sound effects, as both become a subtext to Charlotte's thoughts of comfort which Jerry and Dr. Jaquith might provide. These three statements of the theme amount to minimal exposure for such a striking and characterful melody.

CONCLUSION

The secret of a successful Steiner score is its operation as both written and aural text. There are strong arguments that a film score can never be considered as more than an aural text, existing only in the context of the film that it accompanies and to which, in a post-production conception, it has reacted. Steiner's maxims that the score must always "subordinate itself to the film's drama" and that "every character should have a theme" seem to support this latter contention, sweeping the audience into a fantasy world with wall-to-wall strings and vibraphone, and a tune for every eventuality. His melodies are recognisable, capturing the moment, but their rhythmic and melodic contours prevent one from dwelling on any one idea for too long. As written text, however, the quantity and quality of detail deliberately considered and employed in the score become quite overwhelming, and to dismiss the music as having transitory value only seems incommensurate with Steiner's intentions for it. The attention to connection between themes and melodies, the large and small scale structures, the repetition of particular statements in specific narrative contexts creates a subtext of interpretation which is very obvious on the page; even with the pressure for time under which Steiner must have composed the score, such schemes were clearly important to him and worth designing and employing. But for whose benefit? Despite his professed sincerity about the real value of film music as concert-status music, he was very aware of the musical limitations of the average film-goer, and certainly would not have expected an audience to follow and appreciate his every move, let alone most of them. So perhaps he wrote this score, and others like it, to show what could be done and to meet the criticism that film music is not valid outside its creative context. This is one of the first of the classical thematic scores Steiner wrote which achieved a level of technical potential comparable to that found in the orchestral and textural vibrancy of a contemporary Korngold score, such as *The Sea Hawk* (1940) or *The Adventures of Robin Hood* (1938). So, this could be the score that Steiner wrote to prove himself a great composer to his contemporaries: in bestowing the Academy Award on him for *Now, Voyager*, his peers surely acknowledged this intention.

APPENDIX

Selected film scores by Max Steiner which are structurally or stylistically similar to the score for *Now, Voyager*, with details of Academy Award wins (AA) and nominations (AAN) achieved by Steiner.

1933	*King Kong*		*Virginia City*
1935	*The Informer* (AA)		*All This, and Heaven Too*
1936	*The Charge of the Light Brigade* (AAN)		*A Dispatch from Reuter's*
			The Letter (AAN)
	The Garden of Allah (AAN)		*Santa Fe Trail*
1937	*A Star Is Born*	1941	*The Great Lie*
	The Life of Emile Zola (AAN)		*The Bride Came COD*
			Dive Bomber
1938	*Gold Is Where You Find It* (first film to use the Warner Brothers fanfare, composed by Steiner)		*Sergeant York* (AAN)
		1942	*They Died with Their Boots On*
			In This Our Life
	Jezebel (AAN)		*The Gay Sisters*
	Four Daughters		*Desperate Journey*
	The Dawn Patrol	1943	*Casablanca* (AAN)
1939	*The Oklahoma Kid*		*Watch on the Rhine*
	Dodge City	1944	*Passage to Marseille*
	Dark Victory (AAN)		*The Adventures of Mark Twain* (AAN)
	Daughters Courageous		
	The Old Maid		*Since You Went Away* (AA)
	We Are Not Alone		*Arsenic and Old Lace*
	Gone with the Wind (AAN)	1945	*The Corn Is Green*
1940	*Four Wives*		*Rhapsody in Blue* (AAN)
	Dr Ehrlich's Magic Bullet		*Mildred Pierce*

1946   *Saratoga Trunk*
        A Stolen Life
        Night and Day (AAN)
        The Big Sleep
1947   *Life with Father* (AAN)
        My Wild Irish Rose (AAN)
1948   *The Treasure of the Sierra*
        Madre
        Key Largo
        Johnny Belinda (AAN)
1949   *The Adventures of Don Juan*
        The Fountainhead
        Beyond the Forest (AAN)
        White Heat
1950   *Young Man With a Horn*
        The Flame and The Arrow
        (AAN)
        The Glass Menagerie

NOTES

CHAPTER 1: MAX STEINER'S MUSICAL BACKGROUND

1. Max Steiner, *Notes to You* (Unpublished Autobiography, held as part of the Max Steiner Collection, Arts and Communications Archive, Harold B. Lee Library, Brigham Young University, 1963-65), p. 13.

2. Mosco Carner notes: "Under the directorship of the famous actress Marie Geistinger (1869-75) and her partner and successor, Maximilian Steiner [Max Steiner's grandfather] (1875-80), the theatre enjoyed an immense popularity. It became the home of Viennese operetta where 13 of Strauss's 15 operettas had their first performances between 1871 and 1897." See entry on "Vienna 1830-1945" in Stanley Sadie, ed., *The New Grove Dictionary of Music and Musicians*, Volume 19 (London: Macmillan, 1980), p. 728.

3. Tony Thomas makes this suggestion in his introduction to the "Catalogue of the Max Steiner Collection," and Richard Traubner's account of Maximilian Steiner's career supports this: see James V. D'Arc and Thomas D. Driggs, "Catalogue of the Max Steiner Collection," (Arts and Communications Archive, Harold B. Lee Library, Brigham Young University, 1996), p. 2; Richard Traubner, *Operetta: A Theatrical History* (Oxford: Oxford University Press, 1989), p. 113.

4. Traubner, *Operetta*, p. 113.

5. Steiner, *Notes to You*, p. 16.

6. Steiner, *Notes to You*, p. 14.

7. Steiner, *Notes to You*, p. 14.

8. What Steiner calls the Vienna Imperial Academy in his autobiography was probably called the Konservatorium für Musik und darstellende Kunst when he was a student there. In 1909 it became the Königliche und Kaiserliche Akademie für Musik und darstellende Kunst, giving the title he uses.

9. Steiner, *Notes to You*, p. 17.

10. Steiner, *Notes to You*, p. 18.

11. Steiner, *Notes to You*, p. 18.

12. Traubner, *Operetta*, pp. 296-97.

13. Steiner, *Notes to You*, p. 16.

14. The work is described as an American version of the European operetta style, and its composer was a Viennese born conductor, who became a composer later in his career: see entry on "Operetta," in Sadie, ed., *New Grove Dictionary*, Volume 13, p. 651. Richard Traubner describes *The Belle of New York* as the "first Broadway musical to electrify the West End [in London]." He notes that the debut performance of the operetta in Vienna was in the original German and that the first English performance was in 1901. It is not clear which of these productions Steiner was involved in. See Traubner, *Operetta*, pp. 374-75.

15. Steiner, *Notes to You*, p. 20.

16. Steiner, *Notes to You*, p. 11.

17. Steiner, *Notes to You*, p. 11.

18. For example, in the score for *Now, Voyager*, Steiner asks for a specific number of violins on the main string orchestrated love theme and for a precise combination of percussion instruments for the excursion scene. See the discussion in Chapter 5.

19. Steiner, *Notes to You*, p. 29. This is a fact that I have been unable to corroborate in any other source.

20. See, for example, Richard Traubner, *Operetta*, chapters entitled "The Merry Widow and Her Rivals," pp. 243-74, and "Silver Vienna," pp. 275-302. In *Notes to You*, Steiner recalls being invited to conduct the first London performances of Lehár's *Die lustige Witwe*, however, Edward Leaney, a private researcher, has a copy of the original London production programme of the work, which shows that the musical director was Harold Vicars, who is likely also to have been the conductor. Mr Leaney has reconstructed many of the significant events of Steiner's early years in Vienna and the rest of Europe in a chronology which appears in D'Arc and Driggs, "Catalogue of the Max Steiner Collection," pp. 23-31.

21. A few pages of this survive in the Max Steiner Collection, Box OS15, Folder 2. Other published and short excerpts of unpublished works, including songs and marches for small orchestra, also survive from this time, the earliest dating from 1897, the latest from 1908: Max Steiner Collection, Arts and Communications Archive, Harold B. Lee Library, Brigham Young University, Boxes OS15 and OS16.

22. There was considerable flexibility in the working conditions of musicians in London at this time. Most useful evidence is confined to theatres' own records, which are difficult to access and often incomplete.

23. Steiner, *Notes to You*, pp. 32-43.

24. It appears that Steiner probably went to Paris with the Tiller Girls for the production of *Amsterdam* in 1910, as he gives that date in a consequent anecdote: see Steiner, *Notes to You*, pp. 43-44. Some sheet music for *Killarney* is held in the Unpublished Foreign Music Collection Box OS 16, Folder 13, within the Max Steiner Collection.

25. Steiner, *Notes to You*, pp. 43-44.

26. Steiner, *Notes to You*, pp. 45-46.

27. Steiner, *Notes to You*, pp. 49-50.

28. Steiner, *Notes to You*, p. 55. Steiner describes how his acquaintance with the theatre-loving Duke of Westminster was to prove valuable when he decided to leave for America: see *Notes to You*, pp. 58-59.

29. Chapters XI and XII respectively: see Steiner, *Notes to You*, pp. 62-68 and pp. 69-102.

30. Steiner, *Notes to You*, p. 67.

31. Steiner, *Notes to You*, p. 95. David Raksin describes how Silvers's original idea was adopted by Twentieth Century Fox studio in Roy Prendergast, *Film Music: A Neglected Art*, 2nd Edition (New York: W.W. Norton, 1992), pp. 30-31.

32. Traubner, *Operetta*, p. 377.

33. Steiner, *Notes to You*, p. 69. The best source for information about Steiner's engagements in this period is Ken Bloom's *American Song: The Complete Musical Theatre Companion/1900-1984*, Volumes 1 & 2 (New York: Facts on File Publications, 1985). This comprehensive volume of productions and personnel gives the clearest picture of Steiner's connections, although his autobiography implies a rather lax employment situation.

34. For a list of musicals and theatre productions with which Steiner was involved during this period, see Katherine Daubney, "The View from the Piano: The Film Scores of Max Steiner, 1939-1945" (Unpublished Doctoral Thesis, University of Leeds, 1996), Chapter 3.

35. Possibly *Oui Madame*, which opened in March 1920 and closed off Broadway.

36. Steiner, *Notes to You*, pp. 83, 86.

37. Stanley Green, *The World of Musical Comedy*, 3rd Edition (South Brunswick/New York: A.S. Barnes and Co., 1968), p. 23.

38. Steiner, *Notes to You*, pp. 83-84.

39. Steiner, *Notes to You*, p. 84.

40. Steiner recalls in *Notes to You* that the music was well reviewed, but the show was poor. It lasted four weeks in Philadelphia and Baltimore, but there is some uncertainty about whether it made it to Broadway: Steiner says not, but Tony Thomas says the production had a two-week run. See Tony Thomas, *Film Score: The Art and Craft of Movie Music* (Burbank, California: Riverwood Press, 1991), p. 58. The production does not appear in Bloom, *American Song*. Some of the music Steiner wrote for the show is held in the Max Steiner Collection: there are seven numbers, all of which were published by Harms Music Publishing.

41. Steiner, *Notes to You*, p. 103.

42. Harry Tierney was a popular song composer for Broadway in the early 1920s and took on the role of chief composer for the Ziegfeld Follies in 1924.

43. Steiner, *Notes to You*, p. 104-107

44. Steiner, *Notes to You*, pp. 104-107. Also in Thomas, *Film Score*, pp. 66-67.

45. This score attracted a little critical attention, purely because it existed. See Steiner, *Notes to You*, p. 107.

46. Steiner, *Notes to You*, pp. 118-21.

47. Letter to a fan, dated 11 March 1940, Max Steiner Collection, Box 2, Folder 12.

48. D'Arc and Driggs, "Catalogue of the Max Steiner Collection," p. 19.

CHAPTER 2: STEINER'S TECHNIQUE OF FILM SCORING

1. Hugo Friedhofer discussed his relationship with Steiner in detail in an interview with Irene Kahn Atkins in 1974 for the American Film Institute. He described many late night telephone calls with Steiner to discuss details, but the impression is that Steiner trusted his orchestrator to a high degree. See Linda Danly, ed., *Hugo Friedhofer: The Best Years of His Life*. Scarecrow Filmmakers Series, No. 66 [Series Editor, Anthony

Slide] (Lanham, Maryland and London: The Scarecrow Press, 1999), pp. 27-157.

2. In many cases Steiner composed the title sequence across six staves, although this often depended on the relative complexity of the orchestral effect. For example, the title sequence cue for *Mildred Pierce* (1945) is notated across six staves, because Steiner was dealing with an unusually large number of instruments, including 3 harps and 2 pianos, and percussion, including chimes.

3. Although there are photographs of Steiner conducting the orchestra for a recording session, it is possible that on a project which was rushed for time, the musical director, Leo Forbstein, would have conducted while Steiner carried on with composition of later parts of the score.

4. *Now, Voyager* is typical of those that do not often use key signatures, whereas the scores for *The Gay Sisters* and *Dodge City* both use key signatures for the main themes of the score.

5. A typical example of this is found in *Now, Voyager* score, p. 13. All scores cited in this chapter belong to the archive of Steiner's short scores in the Max Steiner Collection, Arts and Communications Archive, Harold B. Lee Library, Brigham Young University, and are listed in James V. D'Arc and Thomas D. Driggs, "Catalogue of the Max Steiner Collection" (Arts and Communications Archive, Harold B. Lee Library, Brigham Young University, 1996).

6. Steiner, *The Adventures of Mark Twain* score, p. 93.

7. Steiner, *The Adventures of Mark Twain* score, p. 140.

8. Steiner, *Now, Voyager* score, p. 169.

9. Steiner, *The Oklahoma Kid* score, p. 88. Emphasis as in the original.

10. Steiner, *They Died with Their Boots On* score, p. 235.

11. Steiner, *In This Our Life* score, p. 78.

12. Steiner, *In This Our Life* score, p. 120.

13. Steiner, *Mildred Pierce* score, p. 58. W.W. refers to woodwind instruments.

14. Steiner, *Now, Voyager* score, p. 17.

15. Steiner, *Dodge City* score, p. 33.

16. Steiner, *They Died with Their Boots On* score, p. 93.

17. Steiner, *Now, Voyager* score, p. 85.

18. Thomas, *Film Score*, p. 69.

19. Correspondence from David O. Selznick in the Max Steiner Collection, Box 4, Folder 13. Correspondence from Jack L. Warner in the Max Steiner Collection, Box 4, Folder 14. Aljean Harmetz, *Round Up the Usual Suspects: The Making of* Casablanca—*Bogart, Bergman, and World War II* (London: Weidenfeld and Nicolson, 1993), pp. 259-60.

20. Kathryn Kalinak, *Settling the Score: Music and the Classical Hollywood Film* (Madison, Wisconsin: University of Wisconsin Press, 1992), p. 113. This quotation comes originally from an article in the *New York Times*, 29 September 1935.

21. D'Arc and Driggs, "Catalogue of the Max Steiner Collection," p. 10.

22. The use of chromaticism to reflect 'otherness' dates back at least as far as the sixteenth century Italian madrigal, and found frequent employment in the ombra style of eighteenth-century European operatic and instrumental music. More recently feminist musicologists, such as Susan McClary, have explored how chromaticism expresses female sexuality as a form of otherness in the male discourses of nineteenth century opera. See Susan McClary, *Feminine Endings: Music, Gender and Sexuality* (Minneapolis: University of Minnesota Press, 1991) and McClary's chapter, "Narrative Agendas in

'Absolute' Music," in Ruth A. Solie, ed., *Music and Difference: Gender and Sexuality in Music Scholarship* (Berkeley: University of California Press, 1993), pp. 326-44.

23.   Joseph Haydn, Symphony no. 94, Second movement (London: Edition Eulenburg, 1984), p. 26.

24.   A fuller discussion of the circumstances surrounding the use of "As Time Goes By" in Steiner's score can be found in Frank Miller, *Casablanca: As Time Goes By, 50th Anniversary Commemorative* (London: Virgin Books, 1992), p. 160. See also Martin Marks, "Music, Drama, Warner Brothers: The Cases of *Casablanca* and *The Maltese Falcon*," *Michigan Quarterly Review,* Volume 35, Number 1 (Winter 1996); Aljean Harmetz, *Round Up the Usual Suspects: The Making of* Casablanca—*Bogart, Bergman, and World War II* (London: Weidenfeld and Nicolson, 1993).

25.   Steiner, Max, *Notes to You* (Unpublished Autobiography, held as part of the Max Steiner Collection, Arts and Communications Archive, Harold B. Lee Library, Brigham Young University, 1963-65), p. 200.

26.   The lyrics were written by Kim Gannon, and the song became successful after the release of the film, when it was recorded by Dick Haymes. Bette Davis also recorded a version of the song for an album in 1973. See Alan Warner, *Who Sang What on the Screen* (North Ryde, NSW: Angus and Robertson, 1984), p. 61.

27.   For example, *They Died with Their Boots On.*

28.   See, for example, the chapter on Steiner in Mark Evans, *Soundtrack: The Music of the Movies* (New York: Da Capo, 1979).

29.   Steiner, *Notes to You,* pp. 200-201.

30.   Steiner, *Sergeant York* score, p. 27.

31.   Steiner, *Santa Fe Trail* score, p. 39.

32.   Steiner, *Dr. Ehrlich's Magic Bullet* score, p. 2.

33.   Steiner, *Dr. Ehrlich's Magic Bullet* score, p. 43.

34.   Steiner, *Dodge City* score, p. 34.

35.   Steiner, Dr. *Ehrlich's Magic Bullet* score, p. 43.

36. Claudia Gorbman, *Unheard Melodies: Narrative Film Music* (Bloomington/ London: Indiana University Press/British Film Institute, 1987), p. 98, also p. 7. Kathryn Kalinak, *Settling the Score,* p. 134.

37.   *Seattle Times,* 26 January 1941. Taken from the Max Steiner Collection Scrapbooks, Boxes OS8, OS9, OS10.

38.   Steiner, *They Died with Their Boots On* score, p. 17.

39.   Steiner, *Now, Voyager* score, pp. 102-103.

CHAPTER 3: HISTORICAL AND CRITICAL CONTEXT OF *NOW, VOYAGER*

1. Thomas Schatz, *Boom and Bust: The American Cinema in the 1940s* in *History of the American Cinema*, Charles Harpole, general editor, Volume 6 (New York: Charles Scribner's Sons, 1997), p. 49. Schatz provides a detailed summary of production trends across the entire Hollywood system in this period with particular focus on the impact of the war years on American cinema.

2. Maria LaPlace, "Producing and Consuming the Woman's Film: Discursive Struggle in *Now, Voyager*" in Christine Gledhill, ed., *Home is Where the Heart Is: Studies in Melodrama and the Woman's Film* (London: British Film Institute, 1987), pp. 138-39.

3. Thomas Schatz, *The Genius of the System: Hollywood Film Making in the Studio Era* (New York: Pantheon Books, 1988), p. 226. Barry Norman discusses the genre of the 'woman's film' and suggests that it was in part a product of the absence of a significant proportion of the male population at war. He reads the genre as supporting and reinforcing the emancipation of the woman from domestic drudgery, but notes that this freedom was temporary. The corollary to freedom was the notion of loyalty and self-sacrifice, and Norman suggests that films such as *Now, Voyager* presented it with "a fairly heavy hand." See Barry Norman, *Talking Pictures* (London: Arrow Books, 1991), p. 132.

4. LaPlace, "Producing and Consuming the Woman's Film," p. 141. See also Maria LaPlace, "Bette Davis and the Ideal of Consumption: A Look at *Now, Voyager,*" *Wide Angle*, Volume 6, Number 4 (1984), pp. 34-43.

5. LaPlace, "Producing and Consuming the Woman's Film," pp. 141-42.

6. Richard Dyer, *Stars* (London: BFI, 1979), p. 64.

7. *Now, Voyager* Pressbook, p. 2. Archive of Pressbooks, British Film Institute.

8. Jeanine Basinger, *A Woman's View: How Hollywood Spoke to Women 1930-1960* (London: Chatto and Windus, 1993), pp. 438-39.

9. Basinger, *A Woman's View*, p. 13.

10. Jackie Stacey, *Star Gazing: Hollywood Cinema and Female Spectatorship* (London: Routledge, 1994), p. 33.

11. Jeanne Thomas Allen, ed., Introduction to *Now, Voyager*, Wisconsin/Warner Bros. Screenplay Series [Series Editor, Tino Balio] (Madison, Wisconsin: University of Wisconsin Press, 1984), p. 9.

12. LaPlace, "Producing and Consuming the Woman's Film," p. 156.

13. Memo from Olive Higgins Prouty concerning the potential for a screen treatment of her novel *Now, Voyager*; in Rudy Behlmer, ed., *Inside Warner Brothers 1935-1951* (London: Weidenfeld and Nicolson, 1986), p. 166.

14. Casey Robinson, *Now, Voyager* Screenplay, in Allen, ed., *op. cit.,* Scene 151, p. 159.

15. In her discussion of Stanley Cavell's "Pursuits of Happiness," Marian Keane suggests that Cavell's reading supports this view: "Cavell urges us to see Charlotte's life in the terms she sees it: as a journey whose definitions remain, perhaps curiously, open; an adventure dedicated to self discovery or self-knowledge of an order that brings its own fulfillment." Marian Keane, "The Authority of Connection in Stanley Cavell's *Pursuits of Happiness*," *Popular Film and Television*, Volume 13, Issue 3 (Autumn 1985), p. 145.

16. Robinson, *Now, Voyager* Screenplay, Scene 219, p. 222. In the screenplay this line is shown as "People who love you live here." However, this is not the line delivered by Davis in the film.

17. LaPlace, "Producing and Consuming the Woman's Film," p. 164.

18. Robinson, *Now, Voyager* Screenplay, Scene 219, p. 220.

19. Basinger, *A Woman's View*, p. 57.

20. Basinger, *A Woman's View*, p. 57.

21. Caryl Flinn, *Strains of Utopia: Gender, Nostalgia and Hollywood Film Music* (Princeton, New Jersey: Princeton University Press, 1992), p. 148.

22. *Now, Voyager* Pressbook, pp. 7-17.

23. Barbara Creed, "The Position of Women in Hollywood Melodramas," *Australian Journal of Screen Theory*, Issue 4 (July 1978), pp. 27-31.

24. Richard Corliss, *Talking Pictures* (Newton Abbott, Devon: David and Charles,

1975), p. 289.

25. Dyer, *Stars*, p. 66.

26. Charlotte's description of Elliot to Jaquith is typical of the reserve in their relationship, with little emphasis on the positive and much inference of what might otherwise be: "There are no arguments I can think of why I shouldn't marry him. Most every woman wants a man of her own, a home of her own." Robinson, *Now, Voyager* Screenplay, Scene 154, p. 163.

27. Robinson, *Now, Voyager* Screenplay, Scene 181, p. 184.

28. Robinson, *Now, Voyager* Screenplay, Scene 175, p. 178. Jerry's line in the screenplay is "If you can marry this man and be content," but that is not the line he delivers in the film.

29. R. Barton Palmer, The Successful Failure of Therapy in *Now, Voyager*: The Woman's Picture as Unresponsive Symptom" *Wide Angle*, Volume 8, Number 1 (1986), p. 31.

30. Palmer, "The Successful Failure of Therapy in *Now, Voyager*," p. 31.

31. Palmer, "The Successful Failure of Therapy in *Now, Voyager*," pp. 37-38.

32. Robinson, *Now, Voyager* Screenplay, Scene 65B, p. 107.

33. Article entitled "Bette Shows How Not to Be Glamorous in New Film," in *Now, Voyager* Pressbook, p. 6. Davis's reference to Ilka Chase reflects the influence of Chase's character, Charlotte's sister-in-law, Lisa, on the dowdy Charlotte. Not only does Lisa set up the meeting with Dr Jaquith at the beginning of the film, but she suggests the cruise and clearly helps choose Charlotte's clothes. The Pressbook includes other similar articles and such copy as: "Bette plays herself as a girl of 20, herself as a fat and suppressed young woman with an inferiority complex, and herself as a beautiful woman who 'sails forth to seek and find'"; "Bette Davis was near tears. She saw herself as no woman in the world likes to see herself—25 pounds overweight. . . . Her eyebrows were thick and she wore glasses. . . . Her shoes were sensible." *Now, Voyager* Pressbook advertisers' insert, p. 1.

34. LaPlace, "Bette Davis and the Ideal of Consumption: A Look at *Now, Voyager*," p. 36.

35. Both dialogue quotes from Robinson, *Now, Voyager* Screenplay, Scene 216, p. 216. These lines are not spoken in the film as they appear in the screenplay.

36. Barry Norman notes that in 1939 Davis was being paid $4,000 per week, compared with James Cagney's $12,500 per week. By 1947 she was earning $328,000 a year, and was probably the highest salaried woman in America; this represented an increase of about 50 percent on her weekly wage, but it was still significantly less than Humphrey Bogart's salary of over $460,000. See Barry Norman, *Talking Pictures* (London: Arrow Books, 1991), p. 46.

37. Allen, Introduction to *Now, Voyager* Screenplay, p. 28.

38. Dyer, *Stars*, p. 62.

39. LaPlace, "Producing and Consuming the Woman's Film," p. 155.

40. See Richard Dyer, *Stars*, pp. 64-65 for a brief discussion of the generic 'climb down' of the independent woman in Warner Brothers' films.

41. Memo from Olive Higgins Prouty. In Behlmer, ed., *Inside Warner Brothers 1935-1951*, p. 167.

42. Jaquith announces to Charlotte, "Then isn't it wonderful you know so much better?," in Robinson, *Now, Voyager* Screenplay, Scene 205, p. 202.

43. Flinn, *Strains of Utopia*, p. 142.

44. Jerry's remark in Robinson, *Now, Voyager* Screenplay, Scene 219, p. 220. Charlotte tells Jaquith, "Tina needs me as much as she did a minute ago. I've never been needed before!" *Now, Voyager* Screenplay, Scene 205, p. 204.

45. Robinson, *Now, Voyager* Screenplay, Scene 188, p. 188.

46. Robinson, *Now, Voyager* Screenplay, Scene 191, p. 188.

47. Robinson, *Now, Voyager* Screenplay, Scene 207-8, p. 209.

CHAPTER 4: THE MUSIC AND ITS CONTEXT

1. *Riverside Press*, 13 November 1942.

2. Hans Keller, "Film Music—Some Objections," *Sight and Sound* Volume 15, Number 60 (Winter 1946-47). Also, Hans Keller, "Hollywood Music—Another View," *Sight and Sound* Volume 16, Number 64 (Winter 1947-48).

3. Claudia Gorbman, *Unheard Melodies* (Bloomington/London: Indiana University Press/British Film Institute, 1987), p. 98.

4. These excerpts are taken from Steiner's personal correspondence in the Max Steiner Collection, Arts and Communications Archive, Harold B. Lee Library, Brigham Young University.

5. It is not clear which film Steiner is referring to, although it is possible that, given the fervent reaction of the audience, it was a war film.

6. See Figures 2.3 and 2.5 in Chapter 2 for examples of the themes from these films.

7. Steiner assessed his effort for the score of *Santa Fe Trail* in an interview for the *Seattle Times*, 26 January 1941, part of which has already been quoted in Chapter 2: "'It takes eight thousand notes for Errol Flynn to kill a man,' he said. 'He killed thousand and thousands of men and I wrote millions and millions of notes. Then, when I finished with the battles, I had to write two minutes of Raymond Massey hanging music.' It took six weeks to knock off "Santa Fe Trail." The score of "The Letter," which he thinks is the best job he did in 1940, took three weeks." *Seattle Times*, 26 January 1941.

8. *New York Times*, 29 September 1935.

9. *New York Times*, 29 September 1935.

10. This article first appeared in *Hollywood Spectator* in December 1939, but it can be found reproduced in Richard Harwell, ed., *Gone with the Wind as Book and Film* (Columbia, South Carolina: University of South Carolina Press, 1992), p. 165.

11. Excerpts drawn from Gordon Casson's article in *Progressive Weekly, People's Daily World*, 2 September 1939. The Max Steiner Collection, Scrapbook 1, Box OS8.

12. Excerpts drawn from Gordon Casson's article in *Progressive Weekly, People's Daily World*, 2 September 1939. The Max Steiner Collection, Scrapbook 1, Box OS8.

13. *New York Times*, 29 January 1940.

14. Internal Memorandum from Steiner to Carlyle Jones, Publicity Department, Warner Brothers, dated 11 March 1940. Max Steiner Collection, Box 3, Folder 4.

15. Harry Haun and Geoge Raborn, "Max Steiner Has Scored More Movies than Any Composer Is Ever Likely To Again" *Films in Review*, Volume 12 Number 6 (June/July 1961), pp. 338-51.

16. Tony Thomas, Letter in response to Haun and Raborn article, *op. cit. Films in Review*, Volume 12, no. 7 (August/September 1961), pp. 444-46. See also letters from Clifford McCarty and Jerry Myers in *Films in Review*, Volume 12, Number 8 (October 1961), pp. 509-11.

17. *Picture Reports*, 16 August 1939, Review of *Dust Be My Destiny*.

18. *Hollywood Spectator*, 9 December 1939, Review of *We Are Not Alone*.

19. *Motion Picture Daily*, 13 March 1939, Review of *The Oklahoma Kid*.

20. *Pasadena Star News*, 18 March 1939, Review of *Dark Victory*.

21. *The New York Sun*, 11 April 1939, Review of *Dodge City*.

22. "*Variety* at the Preview," *Variety*, 13 December 1939, Review of *Gone with the Wind*.

23. *Variety*, 20 December 1939, Review of *Gone with the Wind*.

24. *Hollywood Reporter*, 7 April 1942, Review of *In This Our life*.

25. *New York Variety*, 3 June 1942, Review of *The Gay Sisters*.

26. *Washington Star*, 1 August 1942, Review of *The Gay Sisters*.

27. Ussher, in Harwell, ed., *Gone with the Wind as Book and Film*, p. 168.

28. The lecture can be found reproduced in The Max Steiner Collection, Box 4, Folder 14.

29. Gorbman, *Unheard Melodies*, p. 7, and Chapter IV, "Classical Hollywood Practice: The Model of Max Steiner," pp. 70-98.

30. Gorbman, *Unheard Melodies*, p. 73.

31. Gorbman, *Unheard Melodies*, p. 66.

32. William Darby and Jack Du Bois, *American Film Music: Major Composers, Techniques, Trends, 1915-1990* (Jefferson, North Carolina: McFarland and Co., 1990), p. xvi.

33. Darby and Du Bois, *American Film Music*, p. 46.

34. Darby and Du Bois, *American Film Music*, p. xv.

CHAPTER 5: AN ANALYSIS OF THE SCORE

1. Kathryn Kalinak, *Settling the Score: Music and the Classical Hollywood Film* (Madison, Wisconsin: University of Wisconsin Press, 1992), p. 63.

2. Claudia Gorbman, *Unheard Melodies: Narrative Film Music* (Bloomington/London: Indiana University Press/British Film Institute, 1987), pp. 26-27.

3. Steiner entitles the main title theme of *The Oklahoma Kid* as "The 'Cagney' Family Theme" (actor James Cagney has the lead role in the film); for *The Gay Sisters* he makes a note beside the first statement of the main melody: "This is the Gaylord theme — to be used throughout the picture in different ways" (Gaylord is the family name of the eponymous sisters). See Steiner, *The Oklahoma Kid* score, p. 2; Steiner, *The Gay Sisters* score, p. 9.

4. Max Steiner, *Now, Voyager* score, p. 47. This score can be found in the Max Steiner Collection, Arts and Communications Archive, Harold B. Lee Library, Brigham Young University.

5. Steiner, Now, Voyager score, p. 79.

6. Steiner, *Now, Voyager* score, p. 92.

7. Steiner, *Now, Voyager* score, pp. 109-10.

8. Charlotte refers to her secretive existence and is forced to reveal her scrapbook, "the intimate journal of Miss Charlotte Vale." Casey Robinson, *Now, Voyager* Screenplay, Scene 22, pp. 69-70.

9. Casey Robinson, *Now, Voyager* Screenplay, Scene 26, p. 75.

10. Steiner, *Now, Voyager* score, p. 35.

11. Steiner, *Now, Voyager* score, p. 39.

12. Steiner, *Now, Voyager* score, p. 127.

13. Steiner, *Now, Voyager* score, p. 136.

14. Steiner, *Now, Voyager* score, p. 182.

15. Steiner uses this material *come sopra* the scene on the cruise where Charlotte recalls her mother's disapproval of mixing with commercial travellers.

16. Robinson, *Now, Voyager* Screenplay, Scene 160, p. 167.

17. Steiner, *Now, Voyager* score, p. 127.

18. There is an interesting direction in the screenplay at this point: "JERRY (violently): 'Of course it's about us! What would it be?' [Then abruptly he gets up and walks to the front windows, camera panning. From the drawing room now the music has changed. It is no longer jazz, but something semi-classical.]" Robinson, *Now, Voyager* Screenplay, Scene 219, p. 220. In the film the library door is closed and the diegetic music can no longer be heard, but Steiner has placed music exactly as the original screenplay designed it, the orchestral love theme providing the contrast with the diegetic jazz. This shift in idiom is similar to that in the deck scene on the cruise when Charlotte first confesses her breakdown.

19. This section of score begins with Charlotte's line, "And just think, it won't be for this time only." Robinson, *Now, Voyager* Screenplay, Scene 219, p. 222.

BIBLIOGRAPHY

NOW, VOYAGER

Allen, Jeanne Thomas, ed. *Now, Voyager*. Wisconsin/Warner Bros. Screenplay Series [Series Editor, Tino Balio]. Madison, Wisconsin: University of Wisconsin Press, 1984.

Creed, Barbara. "The Position of Women in Hollywood Melodramas." *Australian Journal of Screen Theory*, Issue 4 (July 1978), pp. 27-31.

Keane, Marian "The Authority of Connection in Stanley Cavell's *Pursuits of Happiness.*" *Popular Film and Television* Volume 13, Issue 3 (Autumn 1985), pp. 139-150.

LaPlace, Maria "Bette Davis and the Ideal of Consumption: A Look at *Now, Voyager.*" *Wide Angle*, Volume 6, Number 4 (1984), pp. 34-43.

LaPlace, Maria. "Producing and Consuming the Woman's Film: Discursive Struggle in *Now, Voyager.*" In Christine Gledhill, ed., *Home Is Where the Heart Is: Studies in Melodrama and the Woman's Film*. London: British Film Institute, 1987, pp. 138-66.

Now, Voyager Pressbook. Los Angeles: Vitagraph Inc., 1942 .

Palmer, R. Barton. "The Successful Failure of Therapy in *Now, Voyager*: The Woman's Picture as Unresponsive Symptom." *Wide Angle*, Volume 8, Number 1 (1986), pp. 29-38.

Prouty, Olive Higgins. *Now, Voyager*. Cambridge, Massachusetts: Riverside Press, 1941.

Rhodie, Sam "Semiotic Constraints in *Now,* Voyager." *Australian Journal of Screen Theory*, Issue 4 (July 1978), pp. 19-25.

FILM MUSIC

Books

Atkins, Irene Kahn. *Source Music in Motion Pictures*. Rutherford, New Jersey:

Fairleigh Dickinson University Press, 1983.

Bloom, Ken. *Hollywood Song: The Complete Film and Musical Companion.* New York: Facts on File, 1995.

Brown, Royal S. *Overtones and Undertones: Reading Film Music.* Berkeley, California: University of California Press, 1994.

Danly, Linda, ed. *Hugo Friedhofer: The Best Years of His Life.* Scarecrow Filmmakers Series, No. 66 [Series Editor, Anthony Slide]. Lanham, Maryland and London: The Scarecrow Press, 1999.

Darby, William, and Du Bois, Jack. *American Film Music: Major Composers, Techniques, Trends, 1915-1990.* Jefferson, North Carolina: McFarland and Co., 1990.

Eisler, Hanns. *Composing for the Films.* Oxford: Oxford University Press, 1947.

Evans, Mark. *Soundtrack: The Music of the Movies.* New York: Da Capo, 1979.

Flinn, Caryl. *Strains of Utopia: Gender, Nostalgia and Hollywood Film Music.* Princeton, New Jersey: Princeton University Press, 1992.

Gorbman, Claudia. *Unheard Melodies: Narrative Film Music.* Bloomington/London: Indiana University Press/British Film Institute, 1987.

Kalinak, Kathryn. *Settling the Score: Music and the Classical Hollywood Film.* Madison, Wisconsin: University of Wisconsin Press, 1992.

Karlin, Fred, and Wright, Rayburn. *On the Track: A Guide to Contemporary Film Scoring.* New York: Schirmer Books/Macmillan, 1990.

Lack, Russell. *24 Frames Under: A Buried History of Film Music.* London: Quartet Books, 1997.

Levy, Louis. *Music for the Movies.* London: Sampson Law and Marston, 1948.

London, Kurt. *Film Music.* London: Faber and Faber, 1936.

Manvell, Roger, and Huntley, John. *The Technique of Film Music.* New York: Communication Art Books/Focal Press, 1975.

McCarty, Clifford, ed. *Film Music I.* New York: Garland Publishing, 1989.

Palmer, Christopher. *The Composer in Hollywood.* London: Marion Boyars, 1990.

Prendergast, Roy. *Film Music: A Neglected Art.* 2nd Edition. New York: W.W. Norton, 1992.

Skinner, Frank. *Underscore.* Los Angeles: Skinner Music Co., 1950.

Thomas, Tony. *Music for the Movies.* South Brunswick and New York: Barnes, 1973.

Thomas, Tony. *Film Score: The Art and Craft of Movie Music.* Burbank, California: Riverwood Press, 1991.

Warner, Alan. *Who Sang What on the Screen.* North Ryde, NSW: Angus and Robertson, 1984.

Published Articles

Dagle, Joan, and Kalinak, Kathryn. "The Representation of Race and Sexuality: Visual and Musical Construction in *Gone with the Wind.*" *Postscript,* Volume 13, Issue 2 (Winter/Spring 1994).

Haun, Harry, and Raborn, Geroge. "Max Steiner Has Scored More Movies than Any Composer Is Ever Likely To Again." *Films in Review,* Volume 12, Number 6 (June/July 1961).

Huntley, John. "Film Music." *Sight and Sound,* Volume 12, Number 48 (January 1944).

Keller, Hans. "Film Music—Some Objections." *Sight and Sound,* Volume 15, Number

60 (Winter 1946-47).

Keller, Hans. "A Film Analysis of the Orchestra." *Sight and Sound*, Volume 16, Number 61 (Spring 1947).

Keller, Hans. "Hollywood Music—Another View." *Sight and Sound*, Volume 16, Number 64 (Winter 1947-48).

Marks, Martin. "Music, Drama, Warner Brothers: The Cases of *Casablanca* and *The Maltese Falcon*." *Michigan Quarterly Review*, Volume 35, Number 1 (Winter 1996).

Thomas, Anthony. "Hollywood Music" *Sight and Sound*, Volume 16, Number 63 (Autumn 1947).

Unpublished Works

D'Arc, James V. and Driggs, Thomas D. "Catalogue of the Max Steiner Collection." Arts and Communications Archive, Harold B. Lee Library, Brigham Young University, 1996.

Daubney, Katherine S. "The View From the Piano: The Film Scores of Max Steiner, 1939-1945." Unpublished Doctoral Thesis, University of Leeds, 1996.

Steiner, Max. *Notes to You.* Unpublished Autobiography, held as part of the Max Steiner Collection, Arts and Communications Archive, Harold B. Lee Library, Brigham Young University, 1963-65.

Max Steiner Scrapbooks. Max Steiner Collection, Arts and Communications Archive, Harold B. Lee Library, Brigham Young University. Boxes OS8, OS9, OS10.

FEMINIST FILM CRITICISM

Basinger, Jeanine. *A Woman's View: How Hollywood Spoke to Women 1930-1960.* London: Chatto and Windus, 1994.

Doane, Mary Ann. *The Desire to Desire.* London: Macmillan, 1988.

Gledhill, Christine, ed. *Home Is Where the Heart Is: Studies in Melodrama and the Woman's Film.* London: British Film Institute, 1987.

Haskell, Molly. *From Reverence to Rape: The Treatment of Women in the Movies.* London: New English Library, 1975.

Kaplan, E. Ann. *Women and Film: Both Sides of the Camera.* New York: Methuen, 1983.

Kaplan, E. Ann, ed. *Women in Film Noir.* London: British Film Institute, 1980.

Kuhn, Annette. *The Power of the Image.* London: Routledge Kegan Paul, 1985.

Mayne, Judith. *Cinema and Spectatorship.* London: Routledge, 1993.

Stacey, Jackie. *Star Gazing: Hollywood Cinema and Female Spectatorship.* London: Routledge, 1994.

CONTEXTUAL STUDIES: FILM

Behlmer, Rudy. *Memo from David O. Selznick.* London: Macmillan, 1972.

Behlmer, Rudy. *Inside Warner Brothers 1939-1951.* London: Wiedenfield and Nicholson, 1986.

Brown, Gene, ed. *New York Times Encyclopaedia of Film.* New York: New York Times Books, 1984.

Cavell, Stanley. *Pursuits of Happiness*: *The Hollywood Comedy of Remarriage.* Cambridge, Massachusetts: Harvard University Press, 1981.

Corliss, Richard. *Talking Pictures.* Newton Abbott, Devon: David and Charles, 1975.

Crowther, Bruce. *Hollywood Faction.* London: Columbus Books, 1984.

Culbert, David, ed. *Film and Propaganda in America.* Volumes II and III, World War II. Westport, Connecticut: Greenwood Press, 1990.

Dick, Bernard F. *The Star Spangled Screen: The American World War II Film.* Lexington, Kentucky: University Press of Kentucky, 1985.

Dyer, Richard. *Stars.* London: British Film Institute, 1979.

Freedland, Michael. *The Warner Brothers.* London: Harrap, 1983.

Gomery, Douglas. *The Hollywood Studio System.* London: British Film Institute/Macmillan, 1986.

Grant, Barry Keith. *Film Genre Reader.* Austin, Texas: University of Texas Press, 1986.

Harmetz, Aljean. *Round Up the Usual Suspects: The Making of* Casablanca—*Bogart, Bergman, and World War II.* London: Weidenfeld and Nicolson, 1993.

Harwell, Richard, ed. *Gone with the Wind as Book and Film.* Columbia, South Carolina: University of South Carolina Press, 1992.

Higham, Charles, and Greenberg, Joel. *Hollywood in the Forties.* London: A. Zwemmer, 1968.

Lapsley, Robert, and Westlake, Michael. *Film Theory: An Introduction.* Manchester, England: Manchester University Press, 1988.

Mast, Gerald, and Cohen, Marshall. *Film Theory and Criticism,* 3rd Edition. Oxford: Oxford University Press, 1985.

Miller, Frank. *Casablanca: As Time Goes By, 50th Anniversary Commemorative.* London: Virgin Books, 1992.

Naumberg, Nancy. *We Make the Movies.* London: Faber and Faber, 1937.

Norman, Barry. *Talking Pictures.* London: Arrow Books, 1991.

Osborne, Robert A. *Sixty Years of the Oscar: The Official History of the Academy Awards.* New York: Abbeville Press, 1989.

Rosenberg, Bernard, and Silverstein, Harry. *The Real Tinsel.* London: Macmillan, 1970.

Schatz, Thomas. *The Genius of the System: Hollywood Film Making in the Studio Era.* New York: Pantheon Books, 1988.

Schatz, Thomas. *Boom and Bust: The American Cinema in the 1940s.* Volume 6 of *History of the American Cinema*, Charles Harpole, general editor. New York: Charles Scribner's Sons, 1997.

Sennett, Ted. *Warner Brothers Presents.* New Rochelle, N.Y.: Arlington House, 1971.

Shindler, Colin. *Hollywood Goes to War: Films and American Society 1939-1952.* London: Routledge Kegan Paul, 1979.

Sperling, Cass Warner, and Millner, Cork. *Hollywood Be Thy Name: The Warner Brothers Story.* Rocklin, California: Prima Publishing, 1994.

Variety's Film Reviews. New York: R. R. Bowker, 1983.

Walker, John, ed. *Halliwell's Film* Guide, 8th Edition. London: HarperCollins, 1991.

CONTEXTUAL STUDIES: MUSIC

Bloom, Ken. *American Song: The Complete Musical Theatre Companion/1900-1984*, Volumes 1 & 2. New York: Facts on File Publications, 1985.

Gänzl, Kurt. *The Encyclopaedia of Musical Theatre*, Volumes 1 & 2. Oxford:

Blackwell, 1994.

McClary, Susan. *Feminine Endings: Music, Gender and Sexuality.* Minneapolis: University of Minnesota Press, 1991.

Sadie, Stanley, ed. *The New Grove Dictionary of Music and Musicians.* London: Macmillan, 1980.

Solie, Ruth A., ed. *Music and Difference: Gender and Sexuality in Music Scholarship.* Berkeley: University of California Press, 1993.

Traubner, Richard. *Operetta, A Theatrical History.* Oxford: Oxford University Press, 1989.

INDEX

About the Author

KATE DAUBNEY lectures in music at the University of Leeds.

ISBN 0-313-31253-2

90000>

EAN

9 780313 312533

Coventry University